Penn State Season Records from 1887 through 2015

Year	Coach	Record	Champs	Year	Coach	Record	Champs	Bowl col 2
1887	No coach	2-0		1952	Rip Engle	7–2–1		
1888	No coach	0–2–1		1953	Rip Engle	6-3		
1889	No coach	2.2		1954	Rip Engle	7-2		
1890	No coach	2-2		1955	Rip Engle	5-4		
1891	No coach	6-2		1956	Rip Engle	6-2		
1892	George Hoskins	5-1		1957	Rip Engle	6-3		
1893	George Hoskins	4–1		1958	Rip Engle	6–3-1		
1894	George Hoskins	6-0-1		1959	Rip Engle	9-2		Won Liberty
1895	George Hoskins	2-2-3		1960	Rip Engle	7-3		Won Liberty
1896	Samuel B. Newton	3-4		1961	Rip Engle	8-3		Won Gator
1897	Samuel B. Newton	3-6		1962	Rip Engle	9-2		Won Gator
1898	Samuel B. Newton	6-4		1963	Rip Engle	7-3		
1899	Sam B. Boyle	4-6-1		1964	Rip Engle	6-4		
1900	WM Pop Golden	4-6-1		1965	Rip Engle	5-5		
1901	WM Pop Golden	5-3		1966	Joe Paterno	5-5		
1902	WM Pop Golden	7-3		1967	Joe Paterno	8–2-1		Tied Gator
1903	Daniel A. Reed	5-3		1968	Joe Paterno	11-0		Won Orange
1904	Tom Fennell	6-4		1969	Joe Paterno	11-0		Won Orange
1905	Tom Fennell	8-3		1970	Joe Paterno	7-3		
1906	Tom Fennell	8-1-1		1971	Joe Paterno	11-1		Won Cotton
1907	Tom Fennell	6-4		1972	Joe Paterno	10-2		Lost Sugar
1908	Tom Fennell	5-5		1973	Joe Paterno	12–0		Won Orange
1909	Wm. Hollenback	5-0-2		1974	Joe Paterno	10–2		Won Cotton
1910	Jack Hollenback	5-2-1		1975	Joe Paterno	9-3		Lost Sugar
1911	Wm. Hollenback	8-0-1		1976	Joe Paterno	7-5		Lost Gator
1912	Wm. Hollenback	8-0		1977	Joe Paterno	11–1		Won Fiesta
1913	Wm. Hollenback	2-6		1978	Joe Paterno	11-1		Lost Sugar
1914	Wm. Hollenback	5-3-1		1979	Joe Paterno	8–4		Won Liberty
1915	Dick Harlow	7–2		1980	Joe Paterno	10-2		Won Fiesta
1916	Dick Harlow	8–2		1981	Joe Paterno	10-2		Won Fiesta
1917	Dick Harlow	5-4		1982	Joe Paterno	11-1	Champs	Won Sugar
1918	Hugo F. Bezdek	1-2-1		1983	Joe Paterno	8-4-1		Won Aloha
1919	Hugo F. Bezdek	7-1		1984	Joe Paterno	6–5		
1920	Hugo F. Bezdek	7-0-2		1985	Joe Paterno	11-1		Lost Orange
1921	Hugo F. Bezdek	8-0		1986	Joe Paterno	12-0	Champs	Won Fiesta
1922	Hugo F. Bezdek	8–1–1	L. Rose	1987	Joe Paterno	8–4		Lost Citrus
1923	Hugo F. Bezdek	6-4-1		1988	Joe Paterno	5-6		Won Fiesta
1924	Hugo F. Bezdek	6-3	Champs	1989	Joe Paterno	8-3		Won Holiday
1925	Hugo F. Bezdek	4-4-1		1990	Joe Paterno	9–3		Lost Champs
1926	Hugo F. Bezdek	5-4		1991	Joe Paterno	11–2		Won Fiesta
1927	Hugo F. Bezdek	6-2-1		1992	Joe Paterno	7-5		Lost Champs
1928	Hugo F. Bezdek	3-5-1		1993	Joe Paterno	10-2		Won Citrus
1929	Hugo F. Bezdek	6-3-0	Champs	1994	Joe Paterno	12-0		Won Rose
1930	Bob Higgins	3-4-2	Champs	1995	Joe Paterno	9–3		Won Outback
1931	Bob Higgins	2-8		1996	Joe Paterno	11-2		Won Fiesta
1932	Bob Higgins	2-5		1997	Joe Paterno	9-3		Lost Citrus.
1933	Bob Higgins	3–3–1		1998	Joe Paterno	9-3		Won Outback
1934	Bob Higgins	4-4		1999	Joe Paterno	10-3		Won Alamo
1935	Bob Higgins	4-4		2000	Joe Paterno	5-7		

Penn State's Championship Seasons

Year	Coach	Record		Year	Coach	Record	
1936	Bob Higgins	3-5		2001	Joe Paterno	5-6	
1937	Bob Higgins	5-3		2002	Joe Paterno	9-4	Lost Cap "1"
1938	Bob Higgins	3-4-1		2003	Joe Paterno	3-9	
1939	Bob Higgins	5-1-2		2004	Joe Paterno	4-7	
1940	Bob Higgins	6-1-1		2005	Joe Paterno	11-1	Won Orange
1941	Bob Higgins	7-2		2006	Joe Paterno	9–4	Won Outback
1942	Bob Higgins	6-1-1		2007	Joe Paterno	9-4	Won Alamo
1943	Bob Higgins	5-3-1	Champs	2008	Joe Paterno	11-2	Lost Rose
1944	Bob Higgins	6-3		2009	Joe Paterno	11-2	Won Cap "1"
1945	Bob Higgins	5-3		2010	Joe Paterno	7–6	
1946	Bob Higgins	6-2	Champs	2011	Joe Paterno	8-1	
1947	Bob Higgins	9-0 T Cottn	Champs	2011	Tom Bradley	1-3	Lost TickC
1948	Bob Higgins	7-1-1		2012	Bill O'Brien	8-4	Ineligible
1949	Joe Bedenk	5-4	Champs	2013	Bill O'Brien	7-5	Ineligible
1950	Rip Engle	5-3-1		2014	James Franklin	7-6	Lost Pinstripe
1951	Rip Engle	7–2–1		2015	James Franklin	7-6	Lost FTaxS
Total: 856 Wins		382 L	42 Ties	2016	James Franklin	11-3	Lost Rose

2017 James Franklin 11-2
2018 James Franklin 9-4 lost Citrus Bowl to Kentucky
2018 Won Fiesta Bowl v Washington

Total Wins   887
Total Losses 388
Total Ties   42   * Prior to Overtime Rules
Stats from   1887   * Through August 2018

Penn State's Championship Seasons

PSU's first championship all the way past JoePa's two national championships (1982 and 1986) & 5 undefeated, untied seasons to the James Franklin era

This championship book is written for those of us who love Penn State Football. Others can find their missing information from the bookshelves of those PSU fans who have this book. Despite so may great season records, the last time the Nittany Lions won a national championship was in 1986 and it was against Notre Dame, whose last big national win was in 1988. ND fell hard that year and it was because of the Paterno Boys

Coach Paterno was on the field at PSU for lots of years. Besides the two national championship seasons, JoePa brought in five undefeated and untied seasons which Lions fans call "championships", despite the NCAA. Even before RIp Engle, PSU had many championships. Right from the beginning, Penn State was winning the big games.

In 1982, the Nittany Lions were 11-1 and they defeated big back Herschel Walker and Georgia to give Penn State a long-awited NC. Just 3 yrs later, the Nittany Lions came up short in the Orange Bowl v Barry Switzer's Oklahoma Sooners. But the next year, PSU would be back to play for a NC for another big win. John Schaffer got the job done for PSU using the running of DJ Dozier, and the D was better than ever. PSU has always been as good as it gets and still is.

This book captures the many championship moments in Penn State Football. It covers a lot of ground in football stories before George Hoskins in 1892, and the great immortal Penn State coachesHugo Bezdek, Bob Higgins, Rip Engle, Joe Paternoand now James Franklin. You wont believe all that is in this book and once immersed, you will not be able to put this PSU championship book down.

Brian Kelly

Copyright © August 2018 Brian W. Kelly　　　　Editor: Brian P. Kelly
Penn State's Championship Seasons　　　　Author Brian Kelly

All rights reserved: No part of this book may be reproduced or transmitted in any form, or by any means, electronic or mechanical, including photocopying, recording, scanning, faxing, or by any information storage and retrieval system, without permission from the publisher, LETS GO PUBLISH, in writing.

Disclaimer: Though judicious care was taken throughout the writing and the publication of this work that the information contained herein is accurate, there is no expressed or implied warranty that all information in this book is 100% correct. Therefore, neither LETS GO PUBLISH, nor the author accepts liability for any use of this work.

Trademarks: A number of products and names referenced in this book are trade names and trademarks of their respective companies.

Referenced Material: *Standard Disclaimer: The information in this book has been obtained through personal and third party observations, interviews, and copious research. Where unique information has been provided, or extracted from other sources, those sources are acknowledged within the text of the book itself or in the References area in the front matter. Thus, there are no formal footnotes nor is there a bibliography section. Any picture that does not have a source was taken from various sites on the Internet with no credit attached. If resource owners would like credit in the next printing, please email publisher.*

Published by: ....LETS GO PUBLISH!
Editor in Chief ....Brian P. Kelly
Email: ....info@letsgopublish.com
Web site ....www.letsgopublish.com

Library of Congress Copyright Information Pending
Book Cover Design by **Brian W. Kelly**
Editor—**Brian P. Kelly**

ISBN Information: The International Standard Book Number (ISBN) is a unique machine-readable identification number, which marks any book unmistakably. The ISBN is the clear standard in the book industry. 159 countries and territories are officially ISBN members. The Official ISBN for this book is

978-1-947402-91-1

The price for this work is:..........　　　　　　　　　　　**$ 14.95 USD**

10　　9　　8　　7　　6　　5　　4　　3　　2　　1

Release Date:　　　　　　　　　　　　　　　　　　　August 2019

LETS GO PUBLISH!

Dedication

Monsignor Joseph G. Rauscher

Because he is such a great human being and a caring, dedicated instrument of God, who has tended his flock ahead of his own needs, I dedicate this book to Monsignor Joseph G. Rauscher, for his wonderful 27 years of shepherding of St. Nicholas Parish in Wilkes-Barre. The good Monsignor, who is known as Wyoming Valley's pastor, is a man who has touched thousands of lives and even he admits that the interactions "can blow me away sometimes."

He has most recently been the pastor of St. Nicholas Church, Wilkes-Barre, and in this role, has counseled and assisted people across all boundaries — faith, race, ethnicity, social standing — and all by the standards of an Old Testament, Book of Micah injunction, "Do justly, love mercy, walk humbly with thy God."

"He is a wonderful guy. He is extremely kind. We just love him," said John Anstett, a high school classmate, longtime friend and parishioner at St. Nicholas where the 77-year-old priest had served since 1989. "Even in high school, he cared about everyone, about feelings," Anstett said.

Asked his greatest joy as a priest, Monsignor Rauscher said, "It is how privileged I feel the way so many people trust me, confide in me."

"I see him as the community's priest," said Rabbi Larry Kaplan of Temple Israel. "He is there for anyone in need, and he's always smiling. He makes you feel comfortable."

Monsignor Jack Bendik, pastor of St. John the Evangelist Church in Pittston and a seminary classmate of Monsignor Rauscher, said, "He is the most dedicated priest that I ever met. He has a very inclusive nature. He may be in pain, but he is a great inspiration to me and others."

In addition to his pastoral accomplishments, Monsignor Rauscher is one of the most avid Penn State Football fans. He gets to games whenever he can. He loves the Nittany Lions. He and two of his best friends, and high school classmates, John Anstett and Bill Desciak, love sharing great stories at their annual luncheon renewals. Of course, Penn State and its wonderful football program from over the years is often a main topic. God bless the good Monsignor in his retirement.

Acknowledgments:

I appreciate all the help that I received in putting this book together, along with the 66 other books from the past.

My printed acknowledgments were once so large that book readers needed to navigate too many pages to get to page one of the text. To permit me more flexibility, I put my acknowledgment list online at www.letsgopublish.com. The list of acknowledgments continues to grow. Believe it or not, it once cost about a dollar more to print each book.

Thank you all on the big list in the sky and God bless you all for your help.

Please check out www.letsgopublish.com to read the latest version of my heartfelt acknowledgments updated for this book. Thank you all!

In this book, I received some extra special help from many avid Penn State supporters including Bruce Ikeda, Dennis Grimes, Gerry Rodski, Wily Ky Eyely, Angel Irene McKeown Kelly, Angel Edward Joseph Kelly Sr., Angel Edward Joseph Kelly Jr., Ann Flannery, Angel James Flannery Sr., Mary Daniels, Bill Daniels, Angel Robert Gary Daniels, Angel Sarah Janice Daniels, Angel Punkie Daniels, Joe Kelly, Diane Kelly, Brian P. Kelly, Mike P. Kelly, Katie P. Kelly, Angel Ben Kelly, and Budmund (Buddy) Arthur Kelly.

References

I learned how to write creatively in Grade School at St. Boniface School on Blackman Street. I even enjoyed reading some of my own stuff.

At Meyers High School and King's College and Wilkes-University, I learned how to research, write bibliographies and footnote every non-original thought I might have had. I learned to hate ibid, and op. cit., and I hated assuring that I had all citations written down in the proper sequence. Having to pay attention to details took my desire to write creatively and diminished it with busy work.

I know it is necessary for the world to stop plagiarism so authors and publishers can get paid properly, but for an honest writer, it sure is annoying. I wrote many proposals while with IBM and whenever I needed to cite something, I cited it in place, because my readers, IT Managers, could care less about tracing the vagaries of citations. I always hated to use stilted footnotes, or produce a lengthy, perfectly formatted bibliography. I bet most bibliographies are flawed because even the experts on such drivel do not like the tedium.

I wrote 207 books before this book and several hundred articles which were published by many magazines and newspapers. I choose to cite only when an idea is not mine or when I am quoting, and again, when I cite, I choose to cite in place. The reader does not have to trace strange numbers through strange footnotes and back to bibliography elements that may not be readily accessible or available.

Yet, I would be kidding you, if in a book about the great moments in Penn State Football, I tried to bluff my way into trying to make you think that I knew everything before I began to write anything in this book. I spent as much time researching as writing. I might even call myself an expert of sorts now for all the facts that I have uncovered.

Without any pain on your part you can read this book from cover to cover to enjoy the stories about the many great moments in Penn State Football—and there ae many!

This book is not intended for historians but it does teach a lot of history. It is for regular people of all levels of intelligence. It is for people that want to have a fun read, who like smiling when Penn State Football is the topic. It is for people who love Penn State and perhaps for some PSU haters who want some more facts to bolster their arguments.

There are lots and lots of facts in this book. This book is not for sticklers about the mundane aspects of writing that often cause creative writers to lay bricks or paint houses instead. It is for everyday people like you and I who enjoy Penn State because it is Penn State and who enjoy football because it is football. It is that simple.

When the Nittany Lions play a team and they win or lose, that is a historical fact. To discover such facts, it does not require fundamental or basic research. The University itself copyrights its material but only so it can say "no" if somebody else's creativity affects the university negatively. Even Penn State Dame does not own well-known facts that are readily available about legacies such as John Cappelletti, Bob Higgins, Joe Paterno and many championship seasons.

The championships and the coaches are well known and well defined. So, what? As the author of this book, I care but it is a sports book. I use a judicious approach to assure that I am not throwing the bull when I was present facts.

Nonetheless, this is not a book about heavy math algorithms, or potential advances to the internal combustion engine, or space travel, or the eight elements necessary to find a cure for cancer. So, I refuse to treat this book 100% seriously. If you find a fault with this book, I will fix it. Just tell me about it.

This is a book about sports and sports legends and stories about sporting events that have been recorded seven million times already someplace else. Though I tried for sure to get it all right and I used the work of others to assure so, I bet I made a mistake or two.

What is my remedy for the *harmed* if I have made a mistake? I did not write this book to harm anybody. If I did not write this book, would the *harmed individuals* from the book be unharmed. So, at the very least, I can *unpublish* those parts of the book. If any reader is harmed, let me know, and I will do whatever must be done for all to be OK. There is so much to write about Penn State football that if I must remove a story or two the ones that replace it them will be better.

If somehow, I did not cite a fact that a person owns or a quote somebody once spoke first, it surely was not my intention. If you find any such instances in this work, I will do my best to cite in place before the next printing or take the offensive fact or quote out of the book completely at your pleasure. Just let me know. This book is built for fun, not to create anybody any angst.

It took me about three months originally to write because I had to research and come to some conclusions about the Sandusky travesty. I took a position in my first venture but have removed such topics from this book of championships. If I were to have made sure a thought that I had was not a thought somebody else ever had, this book never would have been completed or the citations pages would exceed the prose.

I used accurate PSU Season summaries from whatever source I could to get the scores of all the games. I verified facts when possible. There are many web sites that have great information and facts. Ironically most internet stories are the same exact stories regardless of who the author might be. While I was writing the book, I wrote down a bunch of Internet references that I show you below and when you finish reading this book, you may click and enjoy them.

My favorite source has been the Penn State Student Magazine called the Collegian, which has been published in one way or another under different names from day one at the university.

While I was writing this book, because I was not sure that my citations within the text would be enough, and I was not producing a bibliography, I copied URLs of areas on the Internet in which I had read articles or had downloaded material and had brought articles or pieces of articles into this book. Hopefully, this will satisfy any request for additional information. Here are the URLs used as references or used for information that I have read that helped me write the book. These are not in any particular sequence:

http://espn.go.com/colleges/psu/notebook/_/page/pennstatealltimefantasydraft

http://www.cbsnews.com/news/has-media-ignored-sex-abuse-in-school/

http://shoebat.com/2014/05/06/sexual-abuse-protestant-churches-catholic/

https://www.pinterest.com/pin/9570217928134808/

http://www.salon.com/2011/11/22/alan_dershowitz_thinks_joe_paterno_was_treated_unfairly/

http://www.statecollege.com/news/local-news/the-origins-of-happy-valley,1466515/

http://usatoday30.usatoday.com/sports/college/football/2012-01-26-1060933973_x.htm

http://articles.mcall.com/2012-01-01/sports/mc-penn-state-1231-20120101_1_wally-triplett-chima-okoli-joe-paterno

http://www.centredaily.com/news/local/education/penn-state/jerry-sandusky/article42834075.html

Jack Ham references

- Didinger, Ray. *Pittsburgh Steelers*. New York: Macmillan Co., Inc., 1974.

- "Dobre Shunka." *Official Site of Pro Football Hall of Fame.* 2007. Pro Football Hall of Fame. 30 Sept. 2007. <http://www.profootballhof.com/history/release.jsp?release_id=765>.
- "Hall of Famers." *National Football Foundation's College Football Hall of Fame.* 2007. College Football Hall of Fame. 28 Oct. 2007. <http://www.collegefootball.org/famersearch.php?id=60020>.
- "Jack Ham." *Official Site of Pro Football Hall of Fame.* 2007. Pro Football Hall of Fame. 30 Sept. 2007. <http://www.profootballhof.com/hof/member.jsp?player_id=86>.
- McCullough, Bob. *My Greatest Day in Football: the Legends of Football Recount Their Greatest Moments.* St. Martin's P, 2001.
- O'Toole, Andrew. *Smiling Irish Eyes, Art Rooney and the Pittsburgh Steelers.* Haworth, NJ: St. Johann P, 2004.
- Rappoport, Ken. *The Pennsylvania State University Nittany Lions, Where Have You Gone?* Champaign, IL: Sports LLC, 2005.
- Russell, Andy. *A Steeler Odyssey.* Champaign, IL: Sports LLC, 1998.

http://www.blackshoediaries.com/2007/6/10/214341/999

http://www.sports-reference.com/cfb/players/franco-harris-1.html

http://www.pennlive.com/sports/index.ssf/2013/10/top_10_penn_state_football_games.html

http://www.collegefootballpoll.com/bowl_history_penn_state.html

http://bleacherreport.com/articles/1066020-penn-state-football-10-greatest-nittany-lions-players-in-nfl-history/page/2

https://en.wikipedia.org/wiki/Lombardi_Award

http://www.nytimes.com/1981/11/29/sports/penn-state-routs-no-1-pitt-48-14-bryant-sets-mark-blackledge-leads-lions.html

http://espn.go.com/colleges/psu/notebook/_/page/pennstatealltimefantasydraft

http://abcnews.go.com/US/joe-paterno-biography-reveals-penn-state-coach-despised/story?id=17043830

http://www.blackshoediaries.com/2007/5/13/221130/292

http://www.framingpaterno.com/betrayal-joe-paterno-chapter-ten-conclusions

Preface:

It looks like with the Big Ten Championship win in 2016, Coach James Franklin has turned the page. He has now established himself as a fine Penn State coach and we all look forward to more of the same in the coming years. Bravo Coach Franklin. The 2017 and 2018 years were also done well. Soon we feel there will be another championship coming to Nittany Lion Country.

This book is all about Penn State Football; its founding; its struggles; its greatness; and its many, many championships, acknowledged and not acknowledged as well as a bunch of "almosts." I love Penn State and I especially love Penn State football from the days of Rip Engle when I was coached by my older brother Ed (RIP) about the PSU nuances to the takeover of the program by the one and only Joe Paterno and on to a fine coach, James Franklin.

People like me, who love Penn State, will not be able to apply any other emotion to this book but love. You will love this book. If you hate Penn State, and you read this book, you may develop a deep affinity for the Blue and White that you will have to explain to your friends.

I like to say that Penn State haters will want their very own copy of this book just for additional ammo to verify the PSU faithful braggadocio. No matter what, PSU as an entity will survive, because its greatness transcends the humans that have helped move it forward. Go Lions!

James Franklin is now the head coach of the Nittany Lions. Franklin is a great coach and I wish him well. Joe Paterno had been Penn State everything for 46 years plus 15 as an assistant. Looking at the records of coaches before and after Paterno, he is clearly in a league by himself. If you take Paterno's record and superimpose it upon any great NCAA program, Penn State will dominate.

Season after season from pre-teen to current age status, I rooted for the Nittany Lions to be National Champions. They had five undefeated seasons in the Paterno years along the way in which they were not declared the champs. To the faithful, they were the champs in those years. Who knows why they were not selected? In 1982 and

1986, PSU won the big one—the National Championship. They earned it. Moreover, those two were uncontested.

This book walks you through the whole PSU journey minus 6 years. Yes, even before PSU's first official game, the Lions had played an unofficial game in which they were victorious in 1881. We tell you about it early in the book. Then, the first season without coaches was in 1887. Think about the struggle without even having a coach.

Few of the PSU seventeen coaches took the team for more than five years but eventually, coaches like Bob Higgins and Rip Engle and finally Joe Paterno came along and together they put lots of years in their tenure and they put PSU on the football map.

Penn State is a long-time football power

One hundred thirty-plus years is a long time to be playing football. The official Penn State Nittany Lions football team was established in 1887. This great and storied football powerhouse represents the Pennsylvania State University in college football. The moniker *Nittany Lions* comes from the notion of the Nittany Mountain Lions, which were once thought to have roamed Mount Nittany, the famous local landmark. In addition to the great teams spanning well over 100 years, we will also stop to talk about PSU traditions such as the Nittany Lion.

Today, the Penn State football team competes in the Big Ten Conference, in the NCAA Division I Football Bowl Subdivision. Coach Joe Paterno worked on the arrangements for PSU to join the Big Ten in 1993 after playing as an Independent college football team from its founding through the 1992 season.

You are going to love this book because it is the perfect read for anybody who loves Penn State and Penn State Football and wants to know more about the most revered athletic program of all time.

Few sports books are a must-read but Brian Kelly's *Great Moments in Penn State Football* will quickly appear at the top of Americas most enjoyable must-read books about sports. Enjoy!

Who is Brian Kelly?

Brian Kelly is one of the leading authors in America with this, his 208th published book. Brian is an outspoken and eloquent expert on a variety of topics and he has also written several hundred articles on topics of interest to Americans.

Most of his early works involved high technology. Later, Brian wrote a number of patriotic books and most recently he has been writing human interest books such as The Wine Diet and Thank you, IBM. His books are always well received. He has also written fifty-nin sports books.

Brian's books are highlighted at www.letsgopublish.com. They are for sale at Amazon. Go to Prian's author page at Amazon to find both Kindle and Paperbackforms of his books.

Amazon.com/author/brianwkelly

The best!

Sincerely,

Brian P. Kelly, Editor in Chief
I am Brian Kelly's eldest son.

Table of Contents

Chapter 1 Introduction to Penn State Football 1
Chapter 2 PSU Launches First Official Football Team 13
Chapter 3: From the Lawn to the Field to the Stadium 17
Chapter 4 The Evolution of Modern Football 25
Chapter 5 Nittany Legacies & Lore 31
Chapter 6 PSU Football – First Six Years 1881-1891 33
Chapter 7 PSU First Football Coach -- George Hoskins 1892-1895 ... 39
Chapter 8 Sam Newton Era 1896-1899 47
Chapter 9 Pop Golden Era 1900-1903 51
Chapter 10 Tom Fennell Era 1904-1908 55
Chapter 11 Hollenback Era 1909-1914 57
Chapter 12 Dick Harlow Era 1915-1917 67
Chapter 13 Hugo Bezdek Era 1918-1929 71
Chapter 14 Bob Higgins Era 1930-1949 81
Chapter 15 Rip Engle Era 1950-1965 97
Chapter 16 Joe Paterno Era 1966 to 1980 105
Chapter 17 Joe Paterno Era 1981 to 1995 137
Chapter 18 Joe Paterno Era 1996 to 2011 179
Chapter 19 Bill O'Brien Era 2012 to 2013 203
Chapter 20 James Franklin Era 2014 -2018+ 211
Other Books by Brian W. Kelly: (amazon.com, and Kindle) 223

About the Author

Brian Kelly retired as an Assistant Professor in the Business Information Technology (BIT) Program at Marywood University, where he also served as the IBM i and Midrange Systems Technical Advisor to the IT Faculty. Kelly designed, developed, and taught many college and professional courses. He continues as a contributing technical editor to a number of technical industry magazines, including "The Four Hundred" and "Four Hundred Guru," published by IT Jungle.

Kelly is a former IBM Senior Systems Engineer. His specialty was problem solving for customers as well as implementing advanced operating systems and software on his client's machines. Brian is the author of 208 books and hundreds of magazine articles. He has been a frequent speaker at technical conferences throughout the United States. His favorite tech book, which he wrote, is *Thank You, IBM*, The Story of how IBM helped today's technology millionaires and billionaires gain their vast fortunes.

Brian was a candidate for the US Congress from Pennsylvania in 2010 and he ran for Mayor in his home town in 2015. He loves Penn State Football, especially championship seasons and has been a Penn State fan all his life.

Chapter 1 Introduction to Penn State Football

PSU football celebrated 130 Years in 2016!

This book continues the celebration of Penn State Football; its founding; its struggles; its greatness; and its great championships. People like me, who love Penn State, will love this book. Penn State Haters will want their own copy just for additional ammo. Yet, it won't help them! Hah!

We begin the rest of the Penn State football story in Chapter 2 on the way to the founding of the PSU football program in 1887.

In defining the format of the book, we chose to use a timetable that is based on a historical chronology. Within this framework, we discuss the great championships in Penn State football history, and there are many more great championships that the pundits over the years have admitted. No book can claim to be able to capture everything, as it would be a never-ending story, but we sure try.

John Cappelletti exemplifies PSU football

John Cappelletti was a great Penn State running back and he is the university's only Heisman trophy winner. He was recruited and mentored by Joe Paterno. Cappelletti was not only a great PSU and Pro football player, he is a wonderful man.

Penn State's only Heisman Trophy winner, John Cappelletti, and members of the 1973 team were honored on the 40th anniversary of their undefeated season, at halftime Saturday at Beaver Stadium. Cappelletti's number 22 was retired.

His younger brother Joey, with whom he had a deep relationship, died of leukemia on April 8, 1976. The bond between the brothers was so strong that they made a TV movie about it called "Something for Joey." Cappelletti was played by Marc Singer. This is a great football story that demonstrates the hugeness of the brothers' bond.

In his senior year. Penn State was scheduled to play West Virginia in late October. The morning of the game, Cappelletti was with his little brother Joey and he asked him what he wanted for his upcoming 11th birthday. Joey replied "I want you to score three touchdowns for me. No, four." In the movie, we learn a lot more than the humble Cappelletti would be telling even his closest friends.

Cappelletti did reveal to a teammate before the game his concerns about his brother's wish: "How am I going to score four touchdowns?" Yet, at the end of the 1st half, he had already scored 3 touchdowns. He had four in the bag.

Coach Paterno was not known for running up the score or padding an individual's already impressive stats. Before John went back on the field, the Coach told him that he had played enough and that he would be on the bench for the second half.

Cappelletti said nothing. He quietly took his seat on the bench like a man. Late in the third quarter, a teammate whispered to Paterno, Joey's wish. Joe Paterno, a softie at heart, shouted "22" on the next PSU possession, and Cappelletti took the field. Cappelletti scored his 4th touchdown on the same possession. John Cappelletti pointed to his brother Joey as he ran off the field.

Joe Paterno loved to help build character as well as skill in his players. And, so he was not much for retiring football jerseys. When Bill O'Brien took over the team, during the 2013 season O'Brien made a big change. While Penn State's only Heisman Trophy winner, John Cappelletti, and members of the 1973 team were honored on the 40th anniversary of their undefeated season, at halftime September 7 at Beaver Stadium, Cappelletti's number 22 was retired. Having to be a Heisman may be a future prerequisite to get a jersey retired at PSU but regardless, the bar at Penn State for retired jerseys is now set very high.

One would expect that if he were asked for his opinion after this commemorative event with Penn State defeating Eastern Michigan 45-7, Joe Paterno would not have blessed it just because that wasn't Joe. One could understand his rationale as being that PSU jerseys could not be retired because with all of the great history of Penn State football players, there would be no numbers left.

I am using this same Paterno idea to help promulgate the notion that nobody can write a book about Penn State football that is all inclusive, because even if it can be written, it would be too big to ever be read. I hoped this book of championships would come in at a little over 200 pages, but if it had, you would not have liked it as much . Read what you can when you can. If you love Penn State, it will be a fun experience.

Penn State has been playing football longer than a whole world of people have been alive. During this period, many long and storied rivalries have been formed on the gridiron. For example, the Nittany Lions have played 18 teams 20 or more times in the 130-year history of the program.

Penn State has fared very well in these rivalries. The Nittany Lions own a winning record against 14 of the 18 team's that they have met 20 or more times.

Seven of those 18 teams were on the 2015 schedule; including Temple (43 meetings), Maryland (37), Ohio State (30), Michigan State (28), Army West Point (25), Rutgers (25) and Illinois (22).

Six of those 18 teams are current members of the Big Ten: Illinois, Iowa, Maryland, Michigan State, Ohio State and Rutgers. Eight teams are/were among the opponents on the 2015 and 2016 schedules.

Penn State has played since 2012 or has a future meeting scheduled with 11 of the 18 teams (All of the FBS teams except Navy). Those opponents include: Army West Point (2015), Illinois (2014-15, '18), Iowa (2016-18), Pitt (2016-19), Syracuse (2012), Temple (2014-16) and West Virginia (2023-24), while the Nittany Lions will meet yearly with Big Ten East Division opponents Maryland, Michigan State, Ohio State and Rutgers.

Thirteen of the 18 programs are currently members of NCAA Division I FBS. Bucknell, Lehigh and Penn are among NCAA Division I FCS, while Gettysburg and Lebanon Valley are Division III programs.

We Are... Penn State!

"We Are...Penn State!" These words are what you hear loud and proud during the whole game. As one side of Beaver Stadium exclaims "WE ARE," the other side responds, "PENN STATE!" Some say that this chant, which has become the emblem that embodies Penn State, began in 1948 when the Penn State football team was set to play against the Southern Methodist University at the Cotton Bowl.

Before game day, SMU wanted to meet with PSU to protest having Penn State's black players play in the game. In response to this request, Penn State Guard and Team Captain Steve Suhey came to the defense of his teammates proclaiming, "We are Penn State. There will be no meetings." Today, the slogan is everywhere in the Penn State community as a sign of strength and pride.

There is another story about the origin of the cheer. Cheerleaders from the 1970 / 1980 period were looking for a lively chant such as Ohio State's and USC's great cheers. They adopted "We Are Penn State" as their beat-all, end-all cheer. From the late 1940's to the 1970's the chant was not a mainstay. Thus, Penn State Historian Lou Prato says it was the latter, not the former that brought us the famous chant. All I know is "We Are Penn State!" Either way it is a fine legacy!

Penn State is a long-time football power

One hundred thirty-two years is a long time to be playing football. The Penn State Nittany Lions football team was established in 1887. This great and storied football powerhouse represents the Pennsylvania State University in college football. The moniker *Nittany Lions* comes from the notion of the Nittany Mountain Lions, which were once thought to have roamed Mount Nittany, the famous local landmark. Soon, we'll tell you more about the Nittany Lion.

Today, the Penn State football team competes in the Big Ten Conference, in the NCAA Division I Football Bowl Subdivision. Coach Joe Paterno worked on the arrangements for PSU to join the Big Ten in 1993 after playing as an Independent college football team from its founding through the 1992 season.

At the present time, we say there are only three independent teams left in the NCAA Division I—the Army Black Knights, the BYU Cougars, and the Notre Dame Fighting Irish. The UMass Minuteman team is expected to go independent very soon. So, there will be just three independents from a time in 1978, less than 40 years ago, when there were 54 independent teams playing college football.

PSU is proud of its closeness to the beautiful Mount Nittany and it celebrates the landmark often at its sporting events by playing a special song on campus entitled "The Nittany Lion." Fans know this song as Hail to the Lion, even though that is not technically the name of the song. The song is reprinted at the end of this chapter for your enjoyment.

As an aside, all PSU sports teams are known as the Nittany Lions except the ladies' basketball team which goes by "The Lady Lions."

Penn State: A great football legacy

Established in 1887, the Nittany Lions football team have achieved numerous on-field successes, the most notable of which include four consensus national championships (in 1911, 1912, 1982 and 1986); three Big Ten Conference Championships (in 1994, 2005 and 2008); and 47 appearances in college bowl games, with a postseason bowl record of 29–16–2. You cannot get much better than that.

The team is also #8 all-time in total-wins, one game behind Oklahoma and Alabama. The Nittany Lions play their home games at Beaver Stadium, which is located on-campus in University Park, Pennsylvania. With an official seating capacity of 106,572, Beaver Stadium is worth talking about all by itself. It is a fitting playing venue for a great football program, and a great university. The team is currently coached by James Franklin

Summary of PSU football:

Penn State's intercollegiate football team was established at a time that American Football was just being shaped. The first official PSU football game was played in 1887 but unofficially, the students had managed to slip in an intercollegiate game of their own in 1881. Football became a permanent part of Penn State life in 1887 but the student players had no coaches. They relied on team captains. The desire to play football helped make all the seasons successful.

The first of seventeen Penn State football coaches was George Hoskins, who was hired in 1892. Having been undefeated in its first unofficial season (2-0), the Penn State team soon became a collegiate powerhouse and football became a part of campus life.

The team made numerous bowl appearances and came to national prominence in the 1950s and 1960s under Coach Rip Engle. Joe Paterno took over as coach in 1966, and guided the Nittany Lions to the most wins by any coach in Division I history, as well as the most bowl appearances, and most bowl wins.

Under Coach Paterno, the squad has won two consensus national championships, in 1982 and 1986, three Big Ten titles, and completed five undefeated seasons. Penn State competed as an independent before joining the Big Ten in 1993. On November 22, 2008, Penn State became the sixth Division I program to win 800 games. Four Penn State coaches -- Dick Harlow, Hugo Bezdek, Bob Higgins, and Joe Paterno -- are in the Football Hall of Fame.

Spring 2016 Press Conference

At his March press conference in spring 2016, Coach Franklin, who took over the team in 2014, got a question, which helped him sum up the notion of expectations and results. The Coach is ready and he is convinced the team is ready but he does not want to appear too optimistic. Here it is right from the Coach's mouth

Press Question for Coach Franklin in March 2016: You said the biggest challenge since you've been here is managing expectations. Is that still a challenge and what level will that be in the coming year? [From http://www.gopsusports.com/**]**

JF: I think it is. I think it's been our biggest challenge. I think it's still our challenge moving forward, because there's still work to be done. I think it's something when you're at a place like Penn State, you have to embrace. I love the fact that we have such high expectations, I do. I love that.

You know, I think obviously me coming in in the opening press conference and even moving forward, I've heard from a number of people that I've been too positive. But I think there's that fine line of, we have to build excitement for the direction of the program and we have to build excitement of where we're going because we're going there. There's signs of it all over the place.

But as fans and as coaches and as players, it doesn't always happen at the rate we want it to happen. And again, at a place like Penn State with the history and the traditions and everything we've been through -- I think that's

part of it. I think everything that we've been through over the last five years, everybody's ready to get back, and I get that, and I appreciate that and I respect that and our players do and our coaches do, as well.

There's so many signs and so many great things heading in the right direction for this program and getting back to the Penn State that everybody wants to see on Saturdays and everybody wants to see at the spring game.

It's going to continue to be a challenge of that fine line of getting people excited and stating all the different things that people should be excited about, and also educating.

Also, educating what's going on in our country and the game of college football what's going on all across the country when it comes to facilitates and recruiting and all those things. It's that fine line between educating where we're at, where we're going and how we're going to get there.

I do know this: The only way we're going to get where we're going is all of us together; that's the players; that's the coaches; that's the campus; that's the community; that's the alumni; that's everybody doing it together. And to be honest with you, 99 percent of everybody has been great. The one percent that isn't, they are loud. They are loud. But that's anywhere. I've had that in every college I've been at.

Our thanks to PSU Sports for the facts.

The proof is in the pudding. PSU has had two more years of pudding with a great 20-6 record getting prepared for a championship in 2019.

The Nittany Lion fight song

"The Nittany Lion" is a the PSU unofficial fight song heaped in Penn State tradition but it is not the official PSU fight song. It is, however, played by the Penn State Blue Band at football games and other sporting events.

During the pre-game show of home football games at Beaver Stadium, it has become part of the traditional Lion fanfare and downfield activities. This song is one of the songs most widely associated with the university. Though it is The Nittany Lion, it is often incorrectly referred to as "Hail to the Lion" (or Lions).

Like clock-work, literally, on Fridays and Saturdays, the clock tower in Penn State's Old Main plays a line of the chorus music at the fifteen-minute mark of each hour, and it adds a line every 15 minutes until the whole chorus is played on the completion of the hour. Such great traditions are a part of the Penn State experience.

The song was composed by 1914 Penn State graduate and former Glee Club member James Leyden in 1919. Leyden also wrote the "Victory" song which is the official PSU fight song. *The Nittany Lion* is a classic number with four verses (with the potential for a fifth verse as Nebraska enters the conference) talking about each of the teams Penn State has played or plays in sports.

The first verse talks solely about Penn State and its mascot, the Nittany Lion, while the second verse (older teams like Pitt, Harvard, Cornell, Princeton, and Penn) and third verse (half of the Big Ten) talk about each of the other schools' mascots and how they pale in comparison to the "mighty Nittany Lion."

Realizing that the song left out Wisconsin, Minnesota, Iowa and Illinois, retired Penn State Alumni Association. Director Roger Williams added a fourth verse this millennium.

Here is the song:

Every college has a legend, *Verse I*

Passed on from year to year,
To which they pledge allegiance

And always cherish dear.
But of all the honored idols,

There's but one that stands the test,
It's the stately Nittany Lion,

The symbol of our best.

This is the Chorus -
Hail to the Lion, Loyal and True.
Hail Alma Mater, with your White and Blue.
Penn State forever, Molder of men,

Fight for her honor, Fight, and Victory again.

Indiana has its Hoosiers,   *Verse II*

Purdue its gold and black.
The Wildcats of Northwestern

And Spartans on attack.
Ohio State has its Buckeyes,

Up north the Wolverines.
But the mighty Nittany Lion's,

The best they've ever seen.   *---Now, sing the chorus again*

There's Pittsburgh with its Panther,   *Verse III*

And Penn her Red and Blue,
Dartmouth with its Indian,

And Yale her Bulldog, too.
There's Princeton with its Tiger,

And Cornell with its Bear.
But speaking now of victory,

We'll get the Lion's share.   *---Now, sing the chorus again*

Roger Williams' verse is commonly sung by the Penn State Glee Club, but is not typically played on the field by the Penn State Blue Band, making it much less known than the previous three.

Minnesota has its Gophers,   *Verse IV*

The Illini with the Spear,
The Badgers of Wisconsin,

And Iowa--never fear!
The Big Ten is our conference:

The nation's best by far.
And the Penn State Nittany Lions,

The Big Ten's shining star!   *---Now, sing the chorus again*

Chapter 2 PSU Launches First Official Football Team

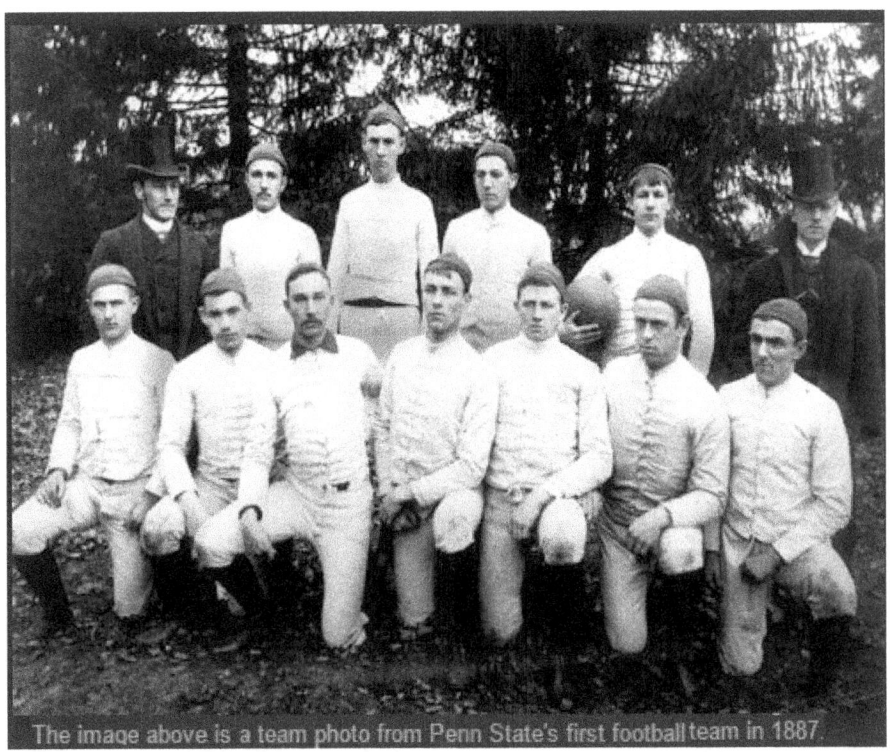

The image above is a team photo from Penn State's first football team in 1887.

1887: Nearly 33 years from the founding

Penn State played its first unofficial football game November 12, 1881 against Lewisburg University in Lewisburg, PA. The Nittany Lions were not yet the Nittany Lions yet they played like they were. Penn State won the makeshift game with rules that were part American football, part rugby, and part soccer as the rules were being incrementally formed. The score was W (9-0).

It was six years later in September (1887) that the School administration gave its approval under President George Atherton. With the top brass's OK; a group of Penn State freshmen organized its first official football team. The architects were freshman George "Lucy" Linsz along with classmate Charles Hildebrand.

Just a month later the storied Penn State tradition began putting notches in its story. Penn State played its first official game November 12, 1887 against Bucknell (formerly Lewisburg) at Lewisburg winning, 54-0. The rules had improved somewhat since 1881 but they were still not the rules of which we are familiar today.

To make it a season and not a shot-in-the dark on-time game as in 1881, Penn State engaged again just one week later on November 19). A mascot-less Penn State played its first home game using a makeshift field on the Old Main lawn. Penn State won the game 24-0 over "rival" Bucknell. Penn State finished its first competitive football season with a 2-0 record. Wins have been the big story in the Penn State football story from 1887 on, and if I may be so bold, unofficially the wins began in 1881.

The notion of college football was just beginning as other Eastern teams such as Harvard and Princeton were also just getting it going. Notre Dame also had its first game in 1887. In 1881, there was a desire to play the evolving game of American football and so the students did it themselves in much the way teams play sandlot football today.

Penn State Students organized a football team without administration support and as noted they scheduled and played a game against a close-by school that at the time was known as the University of Lewisburg (renamed Bucknell University in 1896). The "kids" had to do some research just to know the rules and Penn State learned quite well as it defeated Lewisburg 9-0, in a cold, sleet-like drizzle.

As time moved on from this first encounter with football, there were no more formal games until September 1887 when George "Lucy" Linsz arrived on campus as a freshman and, with the help of a fellow freshman Charles Hildebrand, he managed to get approval from President George Atherton to organize the first official football team for Penn State College. There was no coach and would be no coach for this team until 1894.

As hard as it is to believe back in the fall 1887, Penn State chose Pink and Black as the team colors. They changed the colors to blue and white the following year.

Penn State of course won its first game W (54-0) at Bucknell on the Lewisburg campus. It was the Penn State's first official game. A week later, with no field to speak of, Penn State hosted a home game on the Old Main Lawn. Team Captain and quarterback Lucy Linsz scored three second-half touchdowns to lead Penn State to a 24-0 win over Bucknell. And thus, ended Penn State's first football season.

Chapter 3: From the Lawn to the Field to the Stadium

Beaver Stadium, the home of the Nittany Lions, is one of the nation's premier football venues. An expansion and renovation prior to the 2001 season ad ded more than 12,000 seats, increasing the stadium's capacity to 106,572 and easing the waiting list for season ticket requests from Penn State fans.

When you graduate more than 13,500 students per year university-wide, all of whom love Penn State, is it possible that a stadium holding as many as 500,000 might be insufficient? There are a lot of students and each year, the alumni pool increases by about 13,500. PSU's stadium must be big enough to fit huge crowds

In early 2016, while I was writing this book, Penn State expected to award over 13.500 diplomas to students University-wide who are completing over 500 associates, over 11,000 baccalaureates, over 1,500 master's, over 200law, over 275 doctoral and about 150 medical degrees, bringing the University's total number of graduates to an estimated total of more than 775,000.

At University Park alone, about 9,000 students are expected to be awarded baccalaureate degrees. Approximately 1000 master's degree students are expected to graduate, as are approximately 300 doctoral degree candidates.

Penn State is a fine academic institution and having so many smart people on campus bolsters the opportunity to have a smart football team. PSU football players love playing at Beaver Stadium almost as much as the opposition hates the deafening roar of the eternally optimistic average Penn State fan with a Saturday football ticket.

The "Old Main Lawn" used today for fun

As noted in Chapter2, the first dames were not played in a stadium or a field. They were played on the Old Main Lawn. As you have read, Penn State won its first game W (54-0) at Bucknell on the Lewisburg campus. It was the Penn State's first official game. A week later, with no field to speak of, Penn State hosted a home game on the Old Main Lawn. Team Captain and quarterback Lucy Linsz scored three second-half touchdowns to lead Penn State to a 24-0 win over Bucknell. And thus, ended Penn State's first football season. Things got better over the years with Beaver Stadium now being one of the largest sports-stadium in the world.

Beaver Stadium – A Great Football Venue

Beaver Stadium is the second-largest stadium in the nation and the third largest in the world. Renovations and expansions over the years have added rest rooms and concession facilities, new scoreboards with instant-replay capability, and improved handicap access and pedestrian circulation patterns. The most noticeable recent changes are 60 enclosed skyboxes in a three-level structure above the East stands and an 11,500-seat upper deck in the South end zone.

Beaver Stadium has more than doubled in size since it was relocated from its former site northeast of Rec Hall on the west side of campus to the east end of the campus in 1960. The addition of a 10,033-seat upper deck in the north end zone in 1991 and portable seats on the north end zone concourse increased the stadium's capacity to 93,967.

In 1980, an expansion raised the capacity to 83,770. Lights were added in 1984. In 1985, the addition of walkways around the tops of the end zones and entry ramps at the four corners resulted in lowering the capacity to 83,370.

Today's Beaver Stadium

Penn State dedicated the newly moved and expanded Beaver Stadium with a 20-0 win over Boston University on Sept. 17, 1960.

Nittany Lion halfback Eddie Caye scored the stadium's first touchdown at 10:45 of the first quarter.

Early Beaver Stadium

Built in a horseshoe configuration seating 46,284 in 1960, the stadium now towers 110 rows on the east side, 100 rows on the west, 60 in the lower end zones, 35 in the north upper deck, 20 in the club seating level and 25 in the south upper deck. Most reasonably large cities cannot hold the capacity of Beaver Stadium.

Working from the 1960 move and expansion forward, additions of over 2,000 seats in 1969 and more than 9,000 in 1972 increased the capacity to 57,538. Expanded bleachers in the south end zone in 1976 raised the capacity to 60,203.

A uniquely engineered expansion during the winter, spring and summer of 1978 added more than 16,000 seats, bringing the growing capacity to 76,639. To make this happen, the stadium was cut into sections, raised eight feet by hydraulic jacks and precast concrete seating forms inserted within the inner circle of the stadium, where a running track previously had been located. I bet that one kept the architects and engineers busy figuring out that one.

Before Beaver Stadium, PSU was playing football. Penn State's first permanent home for football was Beaver Field, which stood between the present-day Osmond and Frear laboratories in center campus. Before that, games were played on the Old Main lawn. How about that for scrapping it out?

Old Beaver Field

The first game at 500-seat Beaver Field was played on Nov. 6, 1893 against Western University of Pittsburgh (later to become the University of Pittsburgh). The 32-0 Penn State victory was delayed two days because of bad weather and played on a Monday afternoon.

New Beaver Field, located near Rec Hall, was dedicated in 1909 with a 31-0 win over Grove City. Originally constructed of wood, the stadium was converted to steel in 1936. The area also contained facilities for baseball, lacrosse, soccer and track.

New Beaver Field was the Lions' home through the 1959 season, after which the 30,000-seat stadium was dismantled and moved in 700 pieces one mile to the east side of campus. The old stadium was reassembled with 16,000 additional seats to form Beaver Stadium.

New Beaver Field

The stadium was and is still named in honor of James A. Beaver. Mr. Beaver was a lawyer in nearby Bellefonte at the outbreak of the Civil War. He enlisted in the Union Army as a second lieutenant and rose to the rank of brigadier general prior to his discharge in 1864. Beaver, who died in 1914, served as a superior court judge, governor of Pennsylvania and president of the University's Board of Trustees. He is credited with being among the most influential leaders in the development of the University at the turn of the century.

Though the field officially holds just under 107,000, the game gatekeepers have been able to cheat a bit in permitting more than the stadium's capacity in to see special games. Well, not exactly! Beaver Stadium's official attendance figures include the press box, suites, bands, ushers and other stadium personnel. Here are the top ten games according to attendance.

Top 10 Beaver Stadium Crowds

#	Attend.	Date	Outcome
1.	110,753	Sept. 14, 2002	Penn State 40, Nebraska 7
2.	110,134	Oct. 27, 2007	Ohio State 37, Penn State 17
3.	110,078	Sept. 8, 2007	Penn State 31, Notre Dame 10

4.	110,033	Nov. 7, 2009	Ohio State 24, Penn State 7
5.	110,017	Oct. 18, 2008	Penn State 46, Michigan 17
6.	110,007	Oct. 14, 2006	Michigan 17, Penn State 10
7.	109,865	Nov. 5, 2005	Penn State 35, Wisconsin 14
8.	109,845	Nov. 22, 2008	Penn State 33, Northwestern 7
9.	109,839	Oct. 8, 2005	Penn State 17, Ohio State 10
10.	109,754	Oct. 13, 2007	Penn State 38, Wisconsin 7

2016 Beaver Stadium Expansion
Thoughts from Pennlive.com

November 5, 2015 STATE COLLEGE, Pa. (AP) — Penn State's athletic director says she would prefer to renovate the university's aging icon, Beaver Stadium, rather than build a new one on campus.

The announcement came Wednesday after Sandy Barbour addressed the Nittany Lion faithful during a town hall meeting organized by Penn State's athletic program.

Barbour also said she wasn't opposed to reducing Beaver -- Stadium's seating capacity as part of a future renovation.

Comments by PSU fans / alums

Here are two PSU fans / alums who offer their opinion on whether the university should invest in a new stadium or invest in an upgrade to the existing Beaver Stadium. These are comments from the Penn Live article snippet shown immediately above.

Kenneth Harper Nov 5, 2015
PSU needs to take a very serious look at building a new stadium. PSU got 55+ years out of this one. In 1960 when the stadium was moved to its current location there was nothing around the stadium but plenty of parking. Over time many buildings, (baseball stadium, visitor center, arena and of course the BJC) were built around the stadium. A new stadium at a new location

with plenty of parking, professional seating, modem bathrooms, food stands and even an all year-round restaurant would be nice.

DTM26 Nov 5, 2015

Having a 107,000-seat stadium is huge asset to this team. I know the critics will say "yeah but we only have ~98,000 a game." Yes, but that will change when we start winning again. And look at games like Rutgers (stripe out) and all the whiteout games, those games make Beaver Stadium the best show in college football, and I'm sure some people won't want to hear this, but the high concentration of people is what makes the whiteouts and stripe outs look so good.

It's a huge recruiting tool to say to a kid "you have a chance to play in the third largest stadium in the WORLD." These fans (all 107,000 of them) make this one of the toughest places to play. Lesser teams (like Rutgers this year) are shaken by the very sight of that many people in one place, they simply aren't prepared for it.

I have no problem upgrading Beaver Stadium, especially in the growing arms race that college football is becoming. Rest rooms, concessions, elevators, a new press box, and general sprucing up are all things that should be considered. If some people want individual seats fine, but do not decrease the capacity one person. I suggest we close the four corners of the stadium and add new seats in all 4 corners.

This will do 2 things: add more seats for the people who want more space (let's not forget that the massive south end zone expansion is made up entirely of individual seats as well), and it will also trap noise making it louder. ANY drop-in capacity will be downgrade. And why would you pay hundreds of millions of dollars on a downgrade? This program is headed in the right direction; let's not go backwards now.

Chapter 4 The Evolution of Modern Football

Yale vs. Columbia

Lots of playing before playing became official

The official agreed upon date for the first American-style college football game is November 6, 1869. If you can find a replay of this game someplace in the heavens, however, you would find it would not look much like football as we know it. But, it was not completely soccer or rugby either.

Before this game, teams were playing a rugby style similar to that played in Britain in the mid-19th century. At the time in the US, a derivative known as association football was also played. In both games, a football is kicked at a goal or run over a line. These styles were based on the varieties of English public school football games. Over time, as noted, the style of "football" play in America continued to evolve.

On November 6, 1869, the first football game in America featured Rutgers and Princeton. Before the teams were even on the field it was being plugged as the first college football game of all time. Penn State did not get a Rugby team until the early 1960's. Nobody at Penn State in 1869, from what I could find, was even thinking about the game of football.

The first game of intercollegiate football was a sporting battle between two neighboring schools on a plot of ground where the present-day Rutgers gymnasium now stands in New Brunswick, N.J. Rutgers won that first game, 6-4.

There were two teams of 25 men each and the rules were rugby-like, but different enough to make it very interesting and enjoyable.

Like today's football, there were many surprises; strategies needed to be employed; determination exhibited, and of course the players required physical prowess.

1st Game Rutgers 6 Princeton 4 College Field, New Brunswick, NJ

At 3 p.m. the 50 combatants as well as 100 spectators gathered on the field. Most sat on a low wooden fence and watched the athletes discard their hats, coats and vests. The players used their suspenders as belts. To give a unique look, Rutgers wore scarlet-colored scarfs, which they converted into turbans. This contrasted them with the bareheaded boys from Princeton.

Two members of each team remained more or less stationary near the opponent's goal in the hopes of being able to slip over and score from unguarded positions. Thus, the present day "sleeper" was conceived. The remaining 23 players were divided into groups of 11 and 12. While the 11 "fielders" lined up in their own territory as defenders, the 12 "bulldogs" carried the battle.

Each score counted as a "game" and 10 games completed the contest. Following each score, the teams changed direction. The ball could be advanced only by kicking or batting it with the feet, hands, heads or sides.

Rutgers put a challenge forward that three games were to be played that year. The first was played at New Brunswick and won by Rutgers. Princeton won the second game, but cries of "over-emphasis" prevented the third game in football's first year when faculties of both institutions protested on the grounds that the games were interfering with student studies.

This is an excerpt of the Rutgers account of the game on its web site. A person named Herbert gave this detailed account of the play in the first game:

"Though smaller on the average, the Rutgers players, as it developed, had ample speed and fine football sense. Receiving the ball, our men formed a perfect interference around it and with short, skillful kicks and dribbles drove it down the field. Taken by surprise, the Princeton men fought valiantly, but in five minutes we had gotten the ball through to our captains on the enemy's goal and S.G. Gano, '71 and G.R. Dixon, '73, neatly kicked it over. None thought of it, so far as I know, but we had without previous plan or thought evolved the play that became famous a few years later as 'the flying wedge'."

"Next period Rutgers bucked, or received the ball, hoping to repeat the flying wedge," Herbert's account continues. "But the first time we formed it Big Mike came charging full upon us. It was our turn for surprise. The Princeton battering ram made no attempt to reach the ball but, forerunner of the interference-breaking ends of today, threw himself into our mass play, bursting us apart, and bowing us over. Time and again Rutgers formed the wedge and charged; as often Big Mike broke it up. And finally, on one of these incredible break-ups a

Princeton bulldog with a long accurate, perhaps lucky kick, sent the ball between the posts for the second score.

It was at this point that a Rutgers professor could stand it no longer. Waving his umbrella at the participants, he shrieked, "You will come to no Christian end!"

Herbert's account of the game continues: "The fifth and sixth goals went to Rutgers. The stars of the latter period of play, in the memory of the players after the lapse of many years, were "Big

Mike" and Large (former State Senator George H. Large of Flemington, another Princeton player) ...

Penn Statedid not get into the football act until the late 1880's. At this time, the rules of rugby kept changing to accommodate the infatuation for the Americanized style of "football" play that would ultimately become the American game of football.

Walter Camp: the father of American football?

Walter Camp was a very well-known rugby player from Yale. In today's world, he would have been characterized as a rugby hero. It was his love of the game, his knowledge of the game as it was played, and his innovative mind that caused him to take the evolution of football even further. He pioneered the changes to the rules of rugby that slowly transformed the sport into the new game of American Football.

The rule changes that were introduced to the rugby and

association style (like soccer) of play were mostly those authored by Camp, who was also a Hopkins School graduate. For his original efforts, Walter Camp today is considered to be the "Father of American Football". Among the important changes brought to the game were the introduction of a line of scrimmage; down-and-distance rules; and the legalization of interference (blocking).

There was no such thing in those days as a forward pass and so the legalization of interference in 1880 football permitted blocking for runners. The forward pass would add another dimension to the game that made it much different than rugby or association football.

Soon after the early football changes, in the late nineteenth and into the early twentieth centuries, more game-play type developments were introduced by college coaches. The list is like a who's who of early American College Football. Coaches, such as Eddie Cochems, Amos Alonzo Stagg, Parke H. Davis, Knute Rockne, John Heisman, and Glenn "Pop" Warner helped introduce and then take advantage of the newly introduced forward pass. College football as well as professional football, were introduced prior to the 20th century. Fans were lured into watching again and again once they saw the game played.

College football especially grew in popularity despite the existence of pro-football. It became the dominant version of the sport of football in the United States. It was this way for the entire first half of the 20th century. Bowl games made the idea of football even more exciting in the college ranks. Rivalries grew and continued and the fans loved it! This great football tradition brought a national audience to college football games that still dominates the sports world today.

This book has little to do with pro-football or any other sport. However, there is no denying that the greatest college football players more often than not eventually found their fortunes in professional football. Pro football can be traced back to the season that Notre Dame brought forth a real football team after a two-year lapse from its last half-Rugby season in 1889. It was 1892 when William "Pudge" Heffelfinger signed a $500 contract to play for the Allegheny Athletic Association against the Pittsburgh Athletic Club.

Twenty-eight years later, the American Professional Football Association was formed. This league changed its name to the National Football League (NFL) just two years later. Eventually, the NFL became the major league of American football. Originally, just a sport played in Midwestern industrial towns in the United States, professional football eventually became a national phenomenon. We all know this because from August to February, in America, many of us are glued to our TV sets or chained to our seats in some of the most intriguing pro-football stadiums in America.

Chapter 5 Nittany Legacies & Lore

The Nittany Lion Shrine
The campus is home to the Nittany Lion Shrine, a likeness of the lion carved into limestone, where students gather for spirit events.

The Nittany Lion

The Nittany Lion mascot often pumps up the crowd at many a Penn State football game at Beaver Stadium. The mascot is not entirely fictional. It has some real and some fictitious parts. The legend of the mascot, however, is all real.

As the story goes The Nittany Lion as Penn State's mascot originated with Harrison D. "Joe" Mason, a member of the Penn State class of 1907. In 1904, while playing a baseball game v Princeton in 1904, Mason and other members of Penn State's baseball team were shown a statue of Princeton's famous Bengal tiger as an indication of the *merciless* treatment they could expect to encounter on the field.

At the time, Penn State had no mascot and so Mason replied to the challenge with an instant fabrication of the Nittany Lion, "fiercest beast of them all." Mason's tale suggested the Nittany Lion could overcome even the tiger. Penn State went on to defeat Princeton that day. Over the next few years, the idea of Mason's "Nittany Lion" caught on and won such widespread support among students, alumni, and fans that there was never any official vote on its adoption.

So, the closest we can come to the truth is that The Nittany Lion is in essence an ordinary mountain lion who lived in the region by Mount Nittany. Ordinary mountain lions were tough beasts for sure and were also known as cougar, puma, panther, and catamount. Mountain lions are creatures that reportedly roamed central Pennsylvania until the 1930's, although unconfirmed sightings continue. By attaching the prefix "Nittany" to this beast, Mason gave Penn State a unique symbol that no other college or university could claim.

The Lion's primary means of attack against the Tiger would be its strong right arm, capable of slaying any foes. This fact is now traditionally exemplified through one-armed push-ups after the team scores a touchdown.

Upon returning to campus from this priceless baseball victory over Princeton, Mason set about making his *invention* a reality. In 1907, this graduating senior wrote the following piece in the student publication "*The Lemon:*"

"Every college the world over of any consequence has a college emblem of some kind—all but The Pennsylvania State College. Why not select for ours the king of beasts—the Lion!! Dignified, courageous, magnificent, the Lion allegorically represents all that our College Spirit should be, so why not 'the Nittany Mountain Lion'? Why cannot State have a kingly, all-conquering Lion as the eternal sentinel?"

Ironically, the Lion came from the mind of a Penn State baseball player, not a football guy. Nonetheless it caught on and has been the mascot for over 100 years. With the exception of the *Lady Lions* basketball team, the Nittany Lion moniker represents all sports at Penn State University

Chapter 6 PSU Football – First Six Years 1881-1891

Six No Coach Years

Year	Coach	Record
1881	Unofficial	1-0
1887	No Coach	2-0
1888	No Coach	0-2-1
1889	No Coach	2-2
1890	No Coach	2-2
1891	No Coach	6-2

PSU 1887 Football Team

1887: PSU's first year of football No coach

Penn State's official football program began in 1887 with a two-game season, both games against Bucknell. The first was played at Bucknell's Lewisburg campus and the second was played at the Old Main Lawn at Penn State's main campus.

Though PSU likes to have its official and unofficial football notions kept separate, the fact is the first game was played against the University of Lewisburg at Lewisburg in 1881. No, it was not official but it was played and played well by PSU. Additionally, the 1881 team in retrospect, has taken credit for the blue and white uniforms, not the pink and black worn by the 1987 team. Ivan P. McCreary made a difference

In 1881, this all got started because a determined student, Ivan P. McCreary decided to set up the game, put a team together, and manage the Penn State boys to victory. Since Walter Camp had not yet formed all of the real rules of American football, the 1881 lads played by a mixture of rules that were part rugby and what at the time was known as American football.

McCreary did not play in the game, but he did umpire (The term used at the time for football officials.) At the end of the game as the story goes, he sent a telegraph 50 miles away to Penn State friends that read "we have met the enemy and they are ours, nine to nothing."

Over time as documents were found that chronicled the day, such as the 1882 edition of the University of Lewisburg Mirror, more information was gleaned about the game. "The State College Team was well uniformed and disciplined whereas our boys ... were up to their dodges."

When the official 1887 team was formed, they had a copy and so they studied the American Football Rulebook. This had been written by the great Walter Camp in 1886 and refined for the 1887 season. The official PSU team was not taught by any other team or organization and so they gained their knowledge of the game from Camp's writings. They had a lot of mettle for sure.

Penn States First National Championship

Camp's rule book from 1887 is still available in a reprint. Walter Camp is known as the Father of American Football. He described in this booklet, the transition of rugby to American Football showing the rules dating to 1876 and the then the current Rules for the 1887 season.

Penn State had a great team but who would have supposed otherwise. They won both games in 1887, one at Lewisburg, 54-0, and the other on the Old Main Lawn on the State College campus, 24-0. The old main lawn was just that, a huge lawn in front of the main building. Thus, from the outset Penn State fielded great teams that gave lickings rather than take them. The 1887 team was one of 13 Penn State teams over the years that were undefeated. There's more .

Can we call it a National Championship. In a way it was Lewisburg was a location in the US with a college that played football. We could probably go out and find a few other teams that might claim an undefeated and untied season in 1887 and then we would call them co-champions. But perhaps we should just admit that they were champions for the games they played but there is no sense of an official championsat the national level for 1887. If there were, we'd fight for a share of the title. You bet.

In 1887, Ivy League Teams such as Princeton and Yale and Penn had been playing forms of American Football, a combination of soccer and rugby since about 1869 with more teams playing each year. A group called the NCF who claims to be official, made a declaration in 1887 that Yale was the national champion. Well, I suspect those before me accepted that so if we choose to accept it, we still can claim that PSU won the Lesisburg Championship as contested by the NCF. I like that. Thank you. After all for its first season, undefeated and untied is not too shabby.

In 1887, football as we know it was not completely defined. Association football, rugby, and even soccer were having a major influence at the time on the college football rules and game play. For its first five years, the soon to be "Nittany Lions," football team had no coach. In fact, the whole idea of Penn State football was so tentative that there was a five-year gap from when the first unofficial season occurred until football was "resumed" in 1887. Once PSU's President made it official, the count to 130+ successful seasons began.

Penn State 1888 Football Team

1888: Penn State Football No Coach

Record 0-2-1; without a coach, Penn State sported its own uniforms of blue and white. In muddy terrain, it was reasonably easy to tell the players from the ground until they were completely coated with mud. In stark contrast to the 1887 team, the 1888 team is the only winless team in Penn State history. Harry Leyden (1887–1889) played quarterback in 1888, and both he and the team would do a much better job in 1889.

The season scores are as follows: October 31, Dickinson at home -- Old Main Lawn T (6-6); November 7, Dickinson away at Carlyle PA (0-16). Late November Lehigh at home -- Old Main Lawn L (0-30.

1889: Penn State Football No Coach

With no coach working in the off-season, it was tough getting scheduled games in those first five years. Penn State played Swarthmore in its first game of the season on and got back on the winning side W (20-6) at home – Old Main Lawn. Next two games were losses at Lafayette L (0-26) and at Lehigh L (0-106).

You read that right. It was surely a record-breaker demonstrating how new the team was to real competition. As the season finale, Bucknell was back and even they were tough but Penn State prevailed W (12-0) in a game played at home on the Old Main Lawn.

PSU 1890 Football Team

1890: Penn State Football No Coach

Penn State played four different teams this year and produced a 2-2 record just as in 1889. They lost on October 10 at University of Pennsylvania L (0–20) and came back just two days later on October 12 and lost at Franklin & Marshall in Lancaster, PA L (0–10).

These were both football games though they were losses. On November 15, Penn State played the Altoona Athletic Association on the Old Main Lawn at State College, PA and won big W (68–0). They capped off the season at the Bellefonte Academy in Bellefonte, PA and came away with a win W (23–0)

1891: Penn State Football No Coach

1891: Still with no head coach, for its fifth season, the team was able to schedule an eight-game season starting with a win on October 2 at Lafayette W (14–4). Then the next day it was off to Lehigh on

October 3 where Penn State lost in a battle of the to-be Nittany Lions against the Mountain Hawks. L (2-24). Even in defeat, PSU was playing much tougher than in their prior three seasons.

PSU traveled for a nice win at Swarthmore on October 17 and won 44–0. On October 24, it was at Franklin for a win W (26–6). Then it was off to Gettysburg on October 27 for a nice win W (18-0). Bucknell began to toughen up and got back on Penn State's schedule for 1891. Penn State lost in a close battle on November 7 L (10-12). After a trip to Dickinson on November 26, Penn State came back with a win as Dickinson forfeited. The next game was a big win at Haverford on December 5, W (58–0).

Penn State was getting so much more mature as a football team that the university thought maybe it was time for a coach. The administration hired George Hoskins at the first football coach.

Back in those days, it was often very tough to get a game so colleges would agree to play prep schools and sometimes even high schools to keep their edge.

Chapter 7 PSU First Football Coach -- George Hoskins 1892-1895

Coach # 1

Year	Coach	Record
1892	George Hoskins	5-1
1893	George Hoskins	4-1
1894	George Hoskins	6-0-1
1895	George Hoskins	2-2-3

Finally, PSU had coaches and scheduled games

Penn State 1892 Football Team with 1st Coach Hoskins in a Tie

Penn State was now established both within the institution and outside with other universities as an independent football school, ready to play a full season and ready to be successful.

The University upped the ante in 1892 by reaching into its finances to hire its first football coach.

Picture shows the disorganization of the game of American football at the time

1894 American Football Game

George "Doc" Hoskins Penn State Coach #1

<<< George Hoskins was hired in 1892 as Pennsylvania State University's first head football coach. He resigned at the end of the 1895 season to become head coach at Bucknell and served a trainer for the Cincinnati Reds Baseball organization.

George "Doc" Hoskins served as Penn State's first head coach, while also a player for the Nittany Lions. A three-year letterman at center, he had been the athletic trainer at Vermont before being appointed Penn State's first director of physical training and first instructor of physical education. His duties included coaching the football team to a PSU # 1-win percentage with a record of 17-4-4.

Hoskins was a great coach for Penn State. His .760 winning percentage ranks highest in school history, surpassing notable coaches such as Joe Paterno, Hugo Bezdek, and Rip Engle

Though a student athlete himself, (he played center), Hoskins was the first head coach of PSU. Thus, Penn State's 1892 football season was its first with a formal head coach. George "Doc" Hoskins was at the helm. He did a fine job in his four years and really gave football a big boost at Penn State.

1892 Penn State Football Season Coach George "Doc" Hoskins

Always looking for a mythical championship that one day would come, the 1892 team record was a very respectable 5-1 for the season, with a 4-1 league record. They began slowly with a first game loss at the University of Pennsylvania, a very tough opponent at the time L (0–20).

Then Penn State played a home game against Wyoming Seminary from Northeastern, PA, which is about three hours from Penn State, and just over the five miles from where I live. "Sem," as we call it was and is still a prep school. I found it interesting that they would play college teams. Many teams of the day, in order to get games would play prep schools and even high schools sometime. Prep schools of course would also play high schools just to get a game. PSU did a great job against SEM, who had traveled to the Old Main Lawn for the game. PSU won the game W (40-0).

The Pittsburgh Athletic Club did not care if you were a college team, pro-team, high school team, or a prep team as they, like every other football team at the time, they were happy just to get a game. They brought their athletic manliness into the Old Main Lawn on October 27, and fought a hard battle but could not score. PSU got a nice W (16-0).

The no-longer pushover Bucknell team came to the Old Main Lawn on November 12 and were beaten soundly but no pushover W (18-0).

After this it was Lafayette W (18-0) and Dickinson W (16-0). Penn State had learned to win and no PSU team ever wanted to lose again after tasting both the thrill of victory and the agony of defeat. Hoskins was a fine coach while he had the reins at PSU

1892 Football Facts / Tradition

This was the first Penn State football championship team. How about that? They were crowned in 1892 having won The Pennsylvania Intercollegiate Foot-Ball Association trophy, edging out Bucknell with a 4-1 league record. George Hoskins was a fine coach.

Bucknell quickly became Penn State's first "football rivalry". During this rivalry, games were often heated and hotly contested. The final game between Penn State and Bucknell was played October 2, 1948, Penn State winning 35-0 at what was called, "New Beaver Field." Penn State finished with a 28-10 record against "rival" Bucknell. World War II was tough on a lot of once successful college football programs and many schools completely dropped the sport during and some after the war was over.

Bucknell continues to compete in football in the Division 1 - Football Championship Subdivision of the NCAA. Over the years, PSU has grown to be about 25 X the size of Bucknell's student enrollment of 3600.

1893 Penn State Football Season Coach George "Doc" Hoskins

The 1893 Penn State Nittany Lions football team represented the Pennsylvania State University. The team was coached by George Hoskins in his second year as head coach. FYI, the school did not adopt the Nittany Lion as its mascot until 1907, and Penn State did not become a university until 1953. Nonetheless, we sometimes intentionally refer to the team as the Nittany Lions, and we refer to the institution as PSU. As long as we all know the facts, we will continue to do so as there are few fact checkers from the 1890's around today to get upset with either reference.

The 1893 football team would be the first to play on Beaver Field, Penn State football's first permanent home.

Undefeated seasons were tough to come by as all teams were in their infancy but some had more money to spend on their programs. PSU began the season at Virginia and came back home with a nice W (6–0). Playing again at U of P in Philadelphia, PSU found this well-oiled machine still just a bit much and were defeated L (6-18).

Penn State had just built its 500-seat stadium named Beaver Field and Pittsburgh came to Beaver Field for the first time and the first game on the new home field. The Nittany Lions prevailed W (32–0). Then it was a game at Bucknell in a high scoring win W (36-18) followed by the Pittsburgh Athletic Club, a tough bunch of independents from the left side of Pennsylvania for a close on W (12-0).

Penn State 1893 Football Team with 1st Coach Hoskins with a hat

1894 Penn State Football Season Coach George "Doc" Hoskins

The 1894 Penn State Nittany Lions football team represented the Pennsylvania State University in the college football season. The team was coached by George Hoskins for the third year and for the second year, PSU played its home games on Beaver Field (not Beaver Stadium) in University Park, Pennsylvania.

This was a very successful season for Hoskins and Penn State, gaining a 6-0-1. Penn State was undefeated and untied just once in a close match at Navy on November 10 at Annapolis. The team got rolling quickly on October 13 against Gettysburg at beaver Field with a really big win W (60-0). Penn State football was in graduate school for sure as they played and beat the once impregnable Lafayette at home on October 20, W (72-0).

The Navy tie came next (6-6 at Navy. Then, with a 2-0-1 record, Penn State rolled through its next four games, which were all away. The margins of victory were not big but the determination to win was well established for Penn State teams. First at Bucknell W (12-6); Then, Washington & Jefferson W (6-0), Followed by Oberlin of Ohio W (9-6), and the last game against the Pittsburgh Athletic Club at Pittsburgh on November 29, right after Thanksgiving W (14-0). There was no championship call but you bet with a record like that the Nittany Lions picked up its share of championship trophies

1895 Penn State Football Season Coach George "Doc" Hoskins

Considering the team played just seven games, which was a typical season in 1895, having played three ties, Penn State's record looks a lot worse than it actually is—2-2-3. The 1895 Penn State Nittany Lions football team represented the Pennsylvania State University in college football and this year, the team tied or lost the close games compared with 1894 when in all cases, they won or tied. The team was coached for the fourth and last year by George Hoskins.

The season started well at home on September 25 with a W (26-0) v Gettysburg. Penn State then travelled to upstate NY to play Cornell at Ithaca and came away with a tie T (0-0). Off to Bucknell for a W (16-0) and it looked like a normal successful year for Coach Hoskins.

Then, on November 9, Penn State traveled to the University of Pennsylvania and played a game at Franklin Field, which had just been dedicated for the Penn Relays in April 1895. Penn State had never beaten Penn at the time and this time, they had a really tough time in defeat L (4-35).

Being down a bit from their first loss in two years, the worst that could happen happened when the Nittany Lions traveled to Pittsburgh to play the Athletic club and for the first time were defeated L (10-11) by the slimmest of margins. Penn State came back from these two losses and scored two ties at Washington & Jefferson T (6-6) and Western Reserve at Cleveland T (8-8).

George Hoskins somehow had some eligibility left as a player. Since many colleges and universities were trying to save a buck on their football programs, many for years had no coaches, and then when they decided to pay for a professional coach, they often picked one of the more seasoned members of the team to coach or they lured another student/coach from another institution to coach at their school.

George Hoskins, we might say was stolen by Pitt as many student coaches were stolen during this early time period in college football. Though a well-respected coach at Penn State, as you will read in the next chapter, when Sam Newton brought his Penn State team to Pittsburgh in 1896, there was a major brawl and coach / player Hoskins was right in the middle of it. He wore out his welcome at Penn State and Hoskins coached just one year at Pitt before he left and went to Bucknell.

Chapter 8 Sam Newton Era 1896-1899

Coach #2 Sam Newton
Coach #3 Sam Boyle

Penn State faced some tough years

1896	Sam Newton	3-4
1897	Sam Newton	3-6
1898	Sam Newton	6-4
1899	Sam Boyle	4-6-1

As you can see, this will be a short chapter as there were no seasons out of the four listed that came close to championship caliber.

1896 Penn State Football Season Coach Samuel Newton

The 1896 Penn State Nittany Lions football team represented the Pennsylvania State University in the 1896 college football season. The team was coached by in his first year by Samuel Newton and it played its home games on Beaver Field in University Park, Pennsylvania. Coach Sam Newton's team was 3-4 for the season.

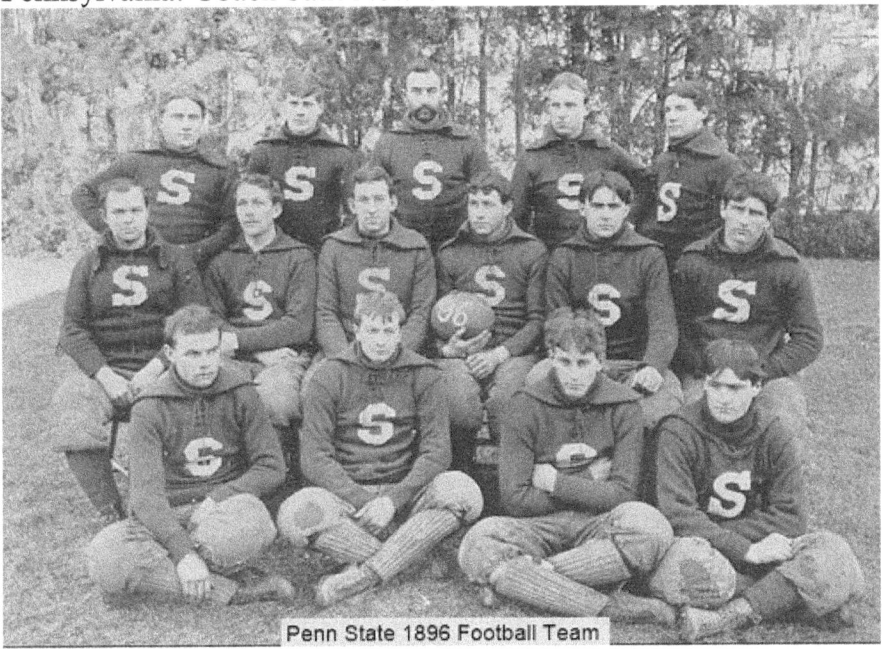
Penn State 1896 Football Team

Sam Newton's gang started off the season with a nice win against Gettysburg W (40-0). This was followed by a trip to Pittsburgh that will be forever remembered in the annals of Penn State Football.

Samuel B. Newton

Newton pictured in *La Vie 1900*, Penn State

When George Hoskins faced Penn State ion October 3, 1896 as a player / coach for Pitt at Beaver Field, he was clearly the enemy. They say from this game on, he was an enemy without any sense of fair play.

The football game became the biggest brawl ever at Beaver Field, and to those watching who covered the game as reporters for the Student Newspaper *Free Lance*, the brawl was instigated as a result of Hoskins' dirty play. Mr. Hoskins impressed none of his one-time admirers that day on Beaver Field. Despite the brawling, Penn State defeated Western PA 10-4 in what was literally a tough game.

According to Free Lance, while playing center and coaching for Western University of Pittsburgh (now Pitt) at Beaver Field where he had coached the prior four years, " he gave such an exhibition of unmanly defiance of all fair rules which degrades the game as to make it a lasting example of the "antis" who hold up to public opinion. This "did more injury to the prestige of the game of football than its promoter can repair."

The four years of great coaching and mentoring that Hoskins had done for Penn State had turned sour. It seems that forgiveness would take a while to bring his good work back into good graces.

1897 Penn State Football Season Coach Samuel Newton

The 1897 Penn State Nittany Lions football team was coached by Samuel Newton and played its home games at Beaver Field in University Park, Pennsylvania. Samuel Newton was in his second year when the 1897 Penn State Nittany Lions football team experienced its second losing season in a row. Coach Sam Newton's team was 3-6 for the season.

1898 Penn State Football Season Coach Samuel Newton

The 1898 Penn State Nittany Lions football team was coached by Samuel Newton in his third and last year as head coach. The team made a great comeback from 1897 with a ten-game schedule, the most in history, and a positive win-loss record at 6-4…but no championship or even an "almost."

1899 Penn State Football Season Coach Sam Boyle (1st Season)

1899 Penn State football team coached by Sam Boyle

It had been a reasonably good season until November with multiple losses starting on November 4 v Bucknell L (0–5). This was followed on Nov. 11 by a tough Yale team at Yale L (0–42). It seemed like PSU would never be able to beat Penn and on Nov. 17 at the continually upgraded Franklin Field in Philadelphia, PA, PSU could not dig out a win (L 0–47). The team finished 4-6-1.

Chapter 9 Pop Golden Era 1900-1903

Coach # 4 Pop Golden
Coach # 5 Daniel A. Reed

Penn State faced some tough years

1900   Pop Golden   4-6-1
1901   Pop Golden   5-3
1902   Pop Golden   7-3
1903   Daniel A. Reed   5-3

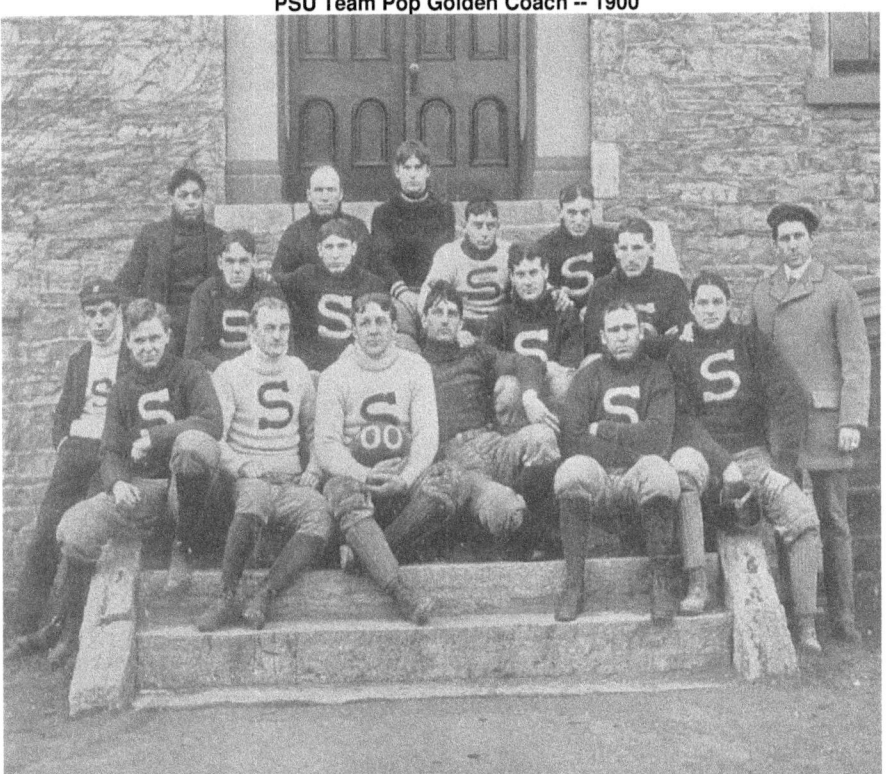

PSU Team Pop Golden Coach -- 1900

1900 Penn State Football Season Coach Pop Golden (1ˢᵗ Season)

The 1900 Penn State Nittany Lions football team was coached by Pop Golden in his first year as head coach. Penn State continued to play its home games at Beaver Field in University Park, Pennsylvania. There were no championships but better records suring Golden's three-year tenure.

Pop Golden (left) won his first game with Penn State on September 23 with a win W (17-0) over Susquehanna at Beaver Field. The team then went to Pittsburgh and won W (12-0) on September 30.

The following week, October 6, at Army in West Point, NY, Penn State tied T (0-0) in a scoreless match.

Next came the Ivy League. First at Princeton; the Tigers defeated PSU handily L 0-26) and on October 17, the Penn Quakers defeated Penn State at Franklin Field L (5-17). It was a lot of games but the Ivy Leaguers were almost incincible at the time.

1901 Penn State Football Season Coach Pop Golden

The 1901 Penn State Nittany Lions football team r was coached by Pop Golden in his second year as head coach. The team played three less games but had a much better record than in 1900, finishing at 5-3.

1902 Penn State Football Season Coach Pop Golden

In 1902, the Penn State Nittany Lions football team were coached for the third and final year by Pop Golden. This was Golden's finest year as the team finished the ten-game season with a very nice 7-3 record.

1903 Penn State Football Season Coach Daniel A. Reed

The 1903 Penn State Nittany Lions football team was coached by Daniel A. Reed in his first and only season as varsity football head coach. The team had a winning season at (5-3)

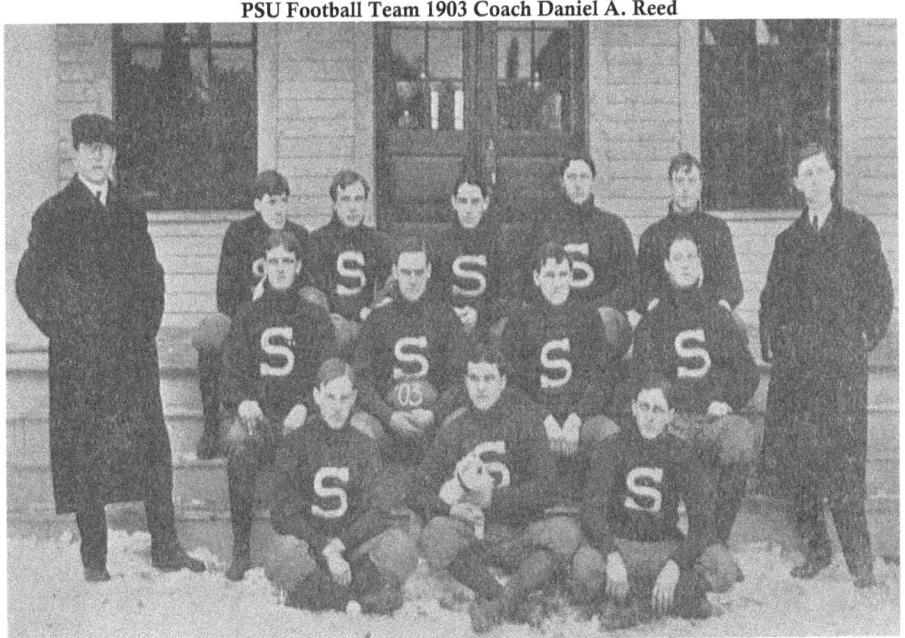

PSU Football Team 1903 Coach Daniel A. Reed

Penn State through 1903 had good fortune in its opening day games, which almost always to this point had doubled as home openers.

Bad fortune was staring Penn State in the face as it made its annual trek to the University of Pennsylvania on October 10 and were defeated again L (0-39.) Yale was the next week at New Haven CT L (0-27). On the brighter side after these two Ivy League teams, Penn State then went to Pittsburgh and soundly won the game W (59-0).

On October 31, PSU trekked to Annapolis to play Navy and won the game W (17-0). Dickinson gave PSU trouble on November 14 and beat Penn State L (0-6). On November 26, Daniel A Reed's team finished the season with a win W (22-0) against Washington & Jefferson in Pittsburgh, PA. And, that's that.

Chapter 10 Tom Fennell Era 1904-1908

Coach # 6

Penn State faced some tough years

1904	Tom Fennell	6-4
1905	Tom Fennell	5-3
1906	Tom Fennell	8-1-1
1907	Tom Fennell	6-4
1908	Tom Fennell	5-5

PSU Football Team 1904 Tom Fennell Coach -- Left

Tom Fennell had all positive records until 1908 when there record was a break-even .500. At 8-1-1, the 1906 team was championship caliber but no Cigar.

Tom Fennell

Fennell pictured in La Vie 1908, Penn State yearbook

1904 Penn State Football Season Coach Tom Fennell

The 1904 Penn State Nittany Lions football team was coached by Tom Fennell in his first season. The team continued to play its home games on Beaver Field in University Park, Pennsylvania. Fennell was coach for five years in total. This year his record was good for a first-year PSU coach at 6-4.

Fennell began his PSU career with a baptism of fire loss against Pennsylvania September 24 at Franklin Field. Penn State to this point had never beaten a Penn team but this time Fennell's team came very close L (0-6). The team sprung right back and defeated

Allegheny at home W (50-0) and then on October 8 lost at Yale L (0-24).

1905 Penn State Football Season Coach Tom Fennell

The 1905 Penn State Nittany Lions football team was coached by Tom Fennell. Their record was 5-3. Soon, in 1907, we will be able to honestly refer to Penn State as the Nittany Lions. In fact, we use PSU all the time but in fact the official university status was not granted until 1953. When we say, PSU, think Penn State. For the record, PSU did not adopt the Nittany Lion as its mascot until 1907. We have two more years to wait until Fennell's fourth year.

1906 Penn State Football Season Coach Tom Fennell

The 1906 Penn State Nittany Lions football team was coached by Tom Fennell for the third year. The team had a great record 8-1-1, with a tie T (0-0) tie against Gettysburg and an away loss at Yale L (0-10).

1907 Penn State Football Season Coach Tom Fennell

The 1907 Penn State Nittany Lions football team was coached by Tom Fennell in his fourth year. This was the first year when Penn State adopted the Nittany Lion as its official mascot. The team finished with a respectable 6-4 record. This was the fourth winning season for Coach Tom Fennell

1908 Penn State Football Season Coach Tom Fennell

The 1908 Penn State Nittany Lions football team was coached by Tom Fennell in his fifth and last season as the head coach of Penn State. Fennel resigned after this season from Penn State and from football. He had the makings of a great coach! The team finished at 5-5 with no championships.

Summary of the Fennell years

Tom Fennell was named Penn State's first full-time head coach in 1904 and compiled a 33-17-1 record in five seasons. He was hired exclusively to coach football and held no additional duties. A graduate of Cornell, where he was a standout in football, Fennell gave up the Penn State post after the 1908 season. He returned to law practice in Elmira, N.Y., and later became a judge. Somehow back then, a judge was a more lucrative position than a football coach.

Chapter 11 Hollenback Era 1909-1914

Coach # 7 Bill Hollenback
Coach # 8 Jack Hollenback

1909	Bill Hollenback	5-0-2
1910	Jack Hollenback	5–2–1
1911	Bill Hollenback	8-0-1
1912	Bill Hollenback	8-0
1913	Bill Hollenback	2-6
1914	Bill Hollenback	5-3-1

*** Produced a few national champions

Though Penn State had some very fine coaches in its early years including Jim Fennell, who figured he would rather be a judge, the notion of Penn State Era coaches really began with Bill Hollenback, who was like a Knute Rockne, though never as celebrated for Penn State. William Marshall "Big Bill" Hollenback was as good as it gets.

PSU Football Team 1909 Coached by Bill Hollenback -Right

His brother Jack, who filled in one year while Bill tested the waters at Missouri was no slouch either. The Hollenback brothers coached the

Penn State Nittany Lions football teams from 1909 to 1914. In Bill's five seasons, he compiled a 28–9–4 record and a .732 winning percentage. Jack Hollenback's team was 5-2-1 with an expected loss v never PSU-beaten Penn and a tough game at Thanksgiving v Pittsburgh. Jack Hollenback could have coached anywhere.

Bill Hollenback's 1911 and 1912 teams were declared national champions. The University was not a university back then and for its own reasons fails to claim these championships. I think they should.

Bill Hollenback's first team after Fennell's 5-5 season was also undefeated with two ties and no recognition but, ladies and gentlemen of the jury, he got no credit for this. He followed a 5-5 coach and went undefeated. Think about how good this guy was in 1909!

Nonetheless it was PSU's first undefeated season in some time. This was a tremendous coach and if we can add his brother as a fine extension, they were as good as it gets in football…ever!

Bill Hollenback, still a kid but a tough kid, nonetheless, trying to find out what the world had to offer, took a ride to the University of Missouri in 1910 to test his mettle and his abilities and to see if what he thought he wanted was what he really wanted. Good for him! What did he know? He intended to find out and did!

He came back to Penn State. Good for us! After making history, and after his brother made history, this great coach made big time history with two consensus national championships that are not on the PSU list. Beaver Field with a capacity of 500 fans at the time, was not big enough to ever pay the other big teams for coming to play. Penn State realized this as all other teams in the US were planning stadium expansions. Before expansions Penn State took on many road trips just to gain major capacity turnouts. With a stadium that could offer real revenue on ticket sales, it would not be long that more teams were coming to University Park and its New Beaver Field (30,000)

Bill Hollenback's teams played all of their home games at the New Beaver Field, which opened in 1909. This field could pay for the whole PSU football program at the time, and because of it, and Bill Hollenback, PSU was able to achieve much more than otherwise.

What a difference a coach makes!

<<< Bill Hollenback If I were a songwriter after writing a few of these great moments' books, I feel I know the difference between good teams and bad teams. I would write a song to the sound of what a difference a day makes and it would be "What a difference a coach makes!" Bill Hollenback (left) was a difference maker. Joe Paterno was also a difference maker!

I played a little football in High School but was never great but I was pretty good in baseball and started in college as a pitcher and had some great games. I had a great coach. I was a great little league coach taking a team that was a non-winner and two out of three years providing championships while all kids played more than the minimum. I coached soccer teams to championships when nobody else could. I knew what to do and I know good coaches know what to do. What a difference a coach makes! Wouldn't we all like to be one?

Tom Fennell was a great coach but maybe he doubted himself about coaching. Who knows! He brought glory to Penn State for sure but maybe he disappointed himself in his last year (5-5) and left the program and became successful because it was in him. He was destined for success…if it were not football, it would be something else…such as the courtroom.

Bill Hollenback was as good a coach as it gets. He was a man with a Paterno spirit. He came back from Missouri to help make Penn State great again!

1909 Penn State Football Season Coach Bill Hollenback

PSU was undefeated and tied once. The 1909 Penn State Nittany Lions football team was coached by Bill Hollenback and for the first time ever played its home games in the New Beaver Field in University Park, Pennsylvania.

The 1909 season went down as one of the most dangerous in the history of college football. The third annual survey by the Chicago Tribune at season's end showed that 10 college players had been killed and 38 seriously injured in 1909, up from six fatalities and 14 maimings in 1908. The nation was beginning to examine changes to college football to make it safer.

The 1909 Games

Bill Hollenback was a stickler for the importance of conditioning and winning. In the first game at Penn State's New Beaver Field against Grove City, Hollenback's newly invigorated Nittany Lions, playing with a new coach and in a new stadium gained a nice victory W (31-0).

Penn State then tied the Carlisle Indians on October 9 in Wilkes-Barre, PA T (8-8). On October 16, the Nittany Lions defeated Geneva at home W (46-0). The next week, Bill Hollenback's team made history against the University of Pennsylvania with a tie T (3-3). This was the first time playing the Quakers at Franklin Field that the Nittany Lions escaped defeat.

The Ivy League was beginning to lose its edge. Previously the "Big Four" (Harvard, Yale, Princeton and Penn) had dominated college football. Just about every year one of these teams was on the Nittany Lions' schedule.

On November 6, The Nittany Lions shut-out Bucknell at Lewisburg W (33-0). On November 12, West Virginia came to New Beaver Field and were defeated soundly W (40-0) Finally, to wrap up the season on what had become a regular Thanksgiving Day game, PSU played Pittsburgh at Forbes Field and defeated their western rivals handily W (37-0). At 5-0-2, Bill Hollenback had brought another undefeated season to Penn State fans but then, he decided to leave for an offer at Missouri. His older brother jack would take the team in 1910.

1910 Penn State Football Season Coach Jack Hollenback

The 1910 Penn State Nittany Lions football team was coached by Jack Hollenback, (picture below) Bill's older brother. Bill had taken a year to test the water outside Pennsylvania.

The Nittany Lions, for the second year, played its home games in New Beaver Field in University Park, Pennsylvania. The team record was very good at 5-2-1. Penn State was operating as an independent school; had no conference affiliations, and had no restrictions on what teams it played.

The Nittany Lions were 5-2-1 in a season which saw admission charged for the first time when Penn State met Bucknell on Nov. 12 at Beaver Field. A Pennsylvania graduate in dentistry, Hollenback also coached at Franklin & Marshall (1908-09) and at the Pennsylvania Military College (Widener) in 1911 before opening a dental practice in Philipsburg, Pa. Brother Bill also had a dentistry degree but opted for football over dentistry. Jack later joined his brother briefly in the coal brokerage business in Philadelphia.

1911 Penn State Football Season Coach Bill Hollenback

The 1911 Penn State Nittany Lions football team was coached by Bill Hollenback, who had succeeded his brother Jack who had succeeded his brother Bill a year earlier. Jack stepped down so his brother could come back to Penn State as its coach after a one-year trek to Missouri. In 1909, Hollenback had an undefeated season with two ties (5-0-2). This year his team produced another undefeated record with just one tie. The team was recognized retroactively as a co-national champion by the National Championship Foundation.

Since there were no national championships per se awarded back in 1911 or 2012; they were awarded post-facto by much respected groups / committees such as the NCF to make life fair, though after the fact. Though nothing really official existed from 1911 and 1912,

Penn State does not appear to refute the claim that this acknowledgment by the NCF is official as do most scribes, pundits and officials. PSU thus has four consensus national championships—1911, 1912 (Bill Hollenback), and 1982 and 1986 (Joe Paterno).

These and other titles, whether shared or solo, which in fact, the NCAA does recognize, one day may be considered official by Penn State University. All things considered, Penn State is more than already halfway to recognizing those titles as the 1911, 1912, 1969, 1982 1986, and 1994 seasons are already showcased on the suites at Beaver Stadium.

1912 Penn State Football Season Coach Bill Hollenback

The 1912 Penn State Nittany Lions football team was coached for the third time in total by Bill Hollenback in his second consecutive year. He had a knack in building a great team and coaching the team to victories. He was the reason for such bug success again for the Nittany Lions for the 1912 college football season. The team had 8 wins and zero losses. It was clearly a championship.

Bill Hollenback brought to State College, the second of Penn State's retrospective national championships. Like the Bill Hollenback teams of 1909 and1911, this team was also undefeated but they were also untied. In fact, this group of players were so good that they were scored upon once (6 points by Cornell). Just the year before the touchdown was worth just five points.

Penn state was led by players Shorty Miller and Pete Mantle. With so many players with M in the last name, that team was knows as the "M" Squad and they hammered out a perfect 8-0 season. At just five feet five inches tall, Shorty Miller was one heck of a football player and a great running back. He was quick and fast and because he had those "little legs," he could stop on a dime, cut and go the other way. He was tough to tackle.

Though short even for the roaring tens, he was also the team's QB and the safety on defense. Miller was a leader. He even returned punts for the Nittany Lions. With his left hand as a unique attribute, Miller threw for a school record nine touchdowns in 1912, a record that stood for over 50 years.

Pete Mantle was the other guy in the backfield and he was big and tough and even tougher to stop. Miller credits him with being the best passer on the team as he could really throw a ball. Mantle was the first PSU player to be indicted into the College hall of Fame. He ran for over 700 yards in this championship season.

Though reasonably close in geography, PSU and OSU had not played each other. The Big Bill Hollenback team of 1912 is known for playing the first of a series of games against eventual rival Ohio State. There is some irony here as Ohio State has always been considered a tough team. Yet, in this Bill Hollenback game, the vaunted Ohioans walked off the field with seven minutes left because Penn State was getting away with unnecessary roughness. The Buckeyes forfeited because of the brutal play of the Nittany Lions once the real score was 37–0. The official score because of the forfeit is 1–0, but the game ball lists the score as 37–0. How about those apples?

Not really trying to be unfair here but facts are facts. The game play of the 1912 team was legendary and tough. Other teams of the era were opting not to play Penn State because of things like shoestring tackles that would put players out of football for a long time, and literally smash-mouth football. PSU gave no team a break during this period but it did hurt their scheduling of subsequent games.

This extremely successful consensus NCF National Championship season began with a win, in the middle there were wins, and at the end, there were more wins. That's all there was—Penn State wins, and plenty of them!

October 5, home, Carnegie Tech, W (41-0); Oct. 12 home New Beaver Field, Washington Jefferson, W (30-0); Oct 19, Percy Field in Ithaca, Cornell, W (29-6); Oct 16, home, Gettysburg, W (25-0); November 2, Franklin Field, Penn, 2nd victory in a row W (14-0); November 9, a slugfest trouncing shutout at home v Villanova W (71-0).

The next two games should have been tough but were not. Bill Hollenback had some magic about destroying the resistance in the opposition. He was quite a coach. On Nov. 16, at OSU, PSU soundly defeated the Buckeyes W (37-0); Then came Thanksgiving on November 28, 1912 at Pittsburgh's Forbes Field. Pitt wished it had played as well as Ohio State but it had not and lost by one additional point W (38-0).

The PSU record was 8-0. It was that simple.

1913 Penn State Football Season Coach Bill Hollenback

The 1913 Penn State Nittany Lions football team was coached by the previously undefeated coach Bill Hollenback. The team was coached by "Big Bill" Hollenback. Following a 26-game unbeaten streak for coach Hollenback (not the program, which had losses in 1910), the Nittany Lions closed out the 1913 season with six straight losses. Hollenback was 26-0-3 going into this season. How could this be? All the losses were close but something was in the wind. Something seemed to happen to the moxie of Bill Hollenback, though, once again, the losses were mostly close. In 1914, he was 5-3-1, a big improvement but, something seemed to be wrong.

PSU started with two wins at home against Carnegie Tech W (49-0) and Gettysburg w (16-0). All of a sudden, the sunlight left the team. Three straight road games brought no victories. Washington & Jefferson L (0-17); Harvard L (0-29) and U of Penn L (0-17). It was as if everybody was waiting for Bill Hollenback for a big payback.

PSU played a new team—Notre Dame at home in a close one (7-14), Navy at Annapolis L (0-10), and of course the season ender at Forbes Field L (6-7). Overall, there were few cheers at PSU in 2013 for the Nittany Lions first losing season with a Hollenback as coach.

A little bit about the Notre Dame game

On November 8, 1913, the Chicago Tribune wrote: "The game was the hardest fought and the most brilliantly played or ever seen at Penn State. With the exception of five minutes each at the close of the first half and the opening of the second half, Penn State outplayed the visitors."

That is how a sportswriter saw the first ever Penn State-Notre Dame game in 1913. In that first game, a stocky, rugged captain by the name of Knute Rockne scored one touchdown to lead the Notre Dame Fighting Irish to a 14-7 win over Penn State in State College. No matter how many times PSU and ND have played over the years, it has been a respectable rivalry.

1914 Penn State Football Season Coach Bill Hollenback

The 1914 Penn State Nittany Lions football team was coached by Bill Hollenback in his fifth and last season with Penn State. Hollenback played a tough season. The games he was supposed to win, he won and the games that were suppose d to be tough, his PSU team lost. I

This season was a lot better than the prior one but perhaps because the home games were more like almost definite wins and the away games were battles. No team expected to get let off the hook easy by a Bill Hollenback coached team. Perhaps the aura of getting whooped by a Hollenback team did not set well with the better teams and when they played Penn State they were better prepared. Let's take a closer look at this last season of Bill Hollenback.

Early on from Sept. 26 on when PSU played Westminster at home, it looked like the Nittany Lions had regained the idea of how to win. Westminster came to Beaver Stadium and upset nothing W (13-0) but the game was close. Muhlenberg appeared at the gate and played in New Beaver Stadium and were defeated but it was still a close game W (22-0).

Gettysburg lined up for Beaver Field next on October 10 and were beaten W (13-0). Ursinas, a new opponent played at beaver stadium and were soundly defeated on October 17, PSU looked like it had gotten its offense back W (30-0). Harvard was next at Allston MA and the results were a tie T (13-13).

Lafayette and Lehigh, two mid-eastern PA tough teams were next on the away schedule and PSU did not fare well, losing on October 31 to Lafayette L (17–0) and on November 7 at Lehigh L (7–20).

On November 13, Michigan State came to New Beaver Field to play the Nittany Lions and they won the very close game L (3-6). The season ended again against a tough Panther team at Pittsburgh's Forbes Field. Penn State lost L (3–13). Though not as disappointing, once you taste undefeated seasons, all losses become somewhat intolerable, though no team can meet that high a bar. The record was

5-3-1, which in any man's league, especially considering the rest of Hollenback's record, it was very respectable.

Chapter 12 Dick Harlow Era 1915-1917

Coach # 9

1915   Dick Harlow   7-2
1916   Dick Harlow   8-2
1917   Dick Harlow   5-4

The World War I Years

1915 Penn State Football Season Coach Dick Harlow

The 1915 Penn State Nittany Lions football team was coached by first year coach Dick Harlow who took over for the retired Bill Hollenback.

Dick Harlow was a tackle on the great PSU teams of 1910 and 1911. The Nittany Lions continued to play home games in New Beaver Field in University Park, PA. Stadium capacity was 30,000, which was nice sized at the time.

Dick Harlow was one heck of a coach and he left way too soon. His forte was in pioneering modern defensive schemes. Because of choice or chance, he would often field undersized teams, and his uniquely coordinated stunts would focus on getting around or between blockers rather than trying to overpower them.

Dick Harlow

Harlow as Penn State boxing coach in 1920

His offenses were based on doing the opposite of what was expected. He used deception and timing rather than power and bulldozing. He used shifts, reverses, and lateral passes. Harlow was one of the great ones. He was honored with an induction into the College Football Hall of Fame as a coach in 1954.

1915 Penn State Football Season Coach Dick Harlow

At 7-2, PSU had a nice record but not championship caliber. The 1915 season began September 15 at home v Westminster. The Lions started the season with a win W (26-0). On October 20, PSU hosted Lebanon Valley W (13-0). Games against Penn were no longer destined to be losses and so this time a PSU played the Quakers in Franklin Field it was a different game W (13-3).

After this road game, Gettysburg came to town W (27-12) followed on October 23 by West Virginia Wesleyan W (28-0). Harvard had become in many ways the nemesis that Penn had been and in a game in Allston MA, the Crimson defeated the Nittany Lions L (0-13). Lehigh was hosted by PSU the following week on Nov. 3, for a nice, hard fought win W (7-0). PSU then traveled to Lafayette in Easton to soundly defeat the Leopards W (33-3). On November 25, the Thanksgiving rivalry was continued at Forbes Field against Pittsburgh. The Panthers prevailed L (0-20).

1916 Penn State Football Season Coach Dick Harlow

The 1916 Penn State Nittany Lions football team was coached by Dick Harlow. They wee 8-2 this year – a fine record.

On September 23, the Nittany Lions began their season at New Beaver Field against Susquehanna with a nice win (27-0). Westminster came to PSU on September 30, were shutout big-time by the Nittany Lions W (55-0). Bucknell came in and scored the first points in 1916 against PSU at home and PSU defeated them in a rout W (50-7). West Virginia Wesleyan came to town on October 14 and left after losing to PSU W (39-0).

Always a tough game, Penn State played Penn at Franklin Field on October 21 in Philadelphia and went home disappointed L (0-15). PSU had its share of home games. This time it was Gettysburg and the Nittany Lions prevailed W (48-2). Geneva came to New Beaver Stadium next on November 4 and hit a revved up Nittany Lions machine in a huge blowout W (79-0).

Lehigh and Lafayette were next. The Lehigh game was played away at Taylor Stadium in Bethlehem and PSU came away with a close win W (10-7). Next was Lafayette at new Beaver Stadium. Lafayette was upset big-time by Penn State W (40-0). Thanksgiving was late this year and so, almost two weeks later Penn State traveled to Forbes Field for the Turkey game rivalry and left disappointed by a big score L 0-31).

Not a bad season for second year coach Dick Harlow, 8-2. No championship but this was a dandy season

1917 Penn State Football Season Coach Dick Harlow

The 1917 Penn State Nittany Lions football team r was coached by Dick Harlow in his third and last season. After two 2-loss seasons, this season was also on the winning side but there were two more losses and less wins because of games played. The Nittany Lions finished at 5-4. Dick Harlow, a fine coach left Penn State after the 1917 season.

Chapter 13 Hugo Bezdek Era 1918-1929

Coach # 10

1918 Hugo Bezdek 1-2-1
1919 Hugo Bezdek 7-1
1920 Hugo Bezdek 7-0-2
1921 Hugo Bezdek 8-0-2
1922 Hugo Bezdek 6-4-1
1923 Hugo Bezdek 6-2-1
1924 Hugo Bezdek 6-3-1
1925 Hugo Bezdek 4-4-1
1926 Hugo Bezdek 5-4-1
1927 Hugo Bezdek 6-2-1
1928 Hugo Bezdek 3-5-1
1929 Hugo Bezdek 6-3

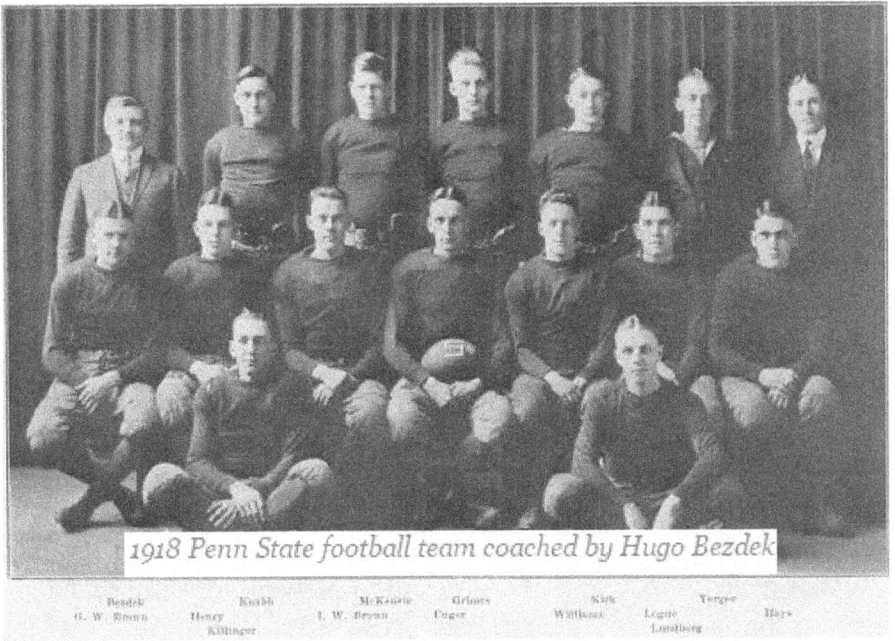

1918 Penn State football team coached by Hugo Bezdek

1918 Penn State Football Season Coach Hugo Bezdek

The 1918 Penn State Nittany Lions football team was coached by Hugo Bezdek in his first year. The high-quality team picture above is from his second-year coaching. Looking back, for sure Bezdek's first season was a strange season right in the heated battles of the war, with just four games and a losing season 1-2-1. It was the worst season in ten years, and one of the worst all-time. Penn State had a tough time getting its season started and when started, it did not do well. World War I was coming to an end.

1919 Penn State Football Season Coach Hugo Bezdek

The 1919 Penn State Nittany Lions football team was coached by Hugo Bezdek. Hugo had really gotten situated as coach and now that the war was over, he was able to build a fine team and they had a great record at 7-1. It was just the one close loss L (13-19) at Dartmouth in New Hampshire that kept the team from a perfect season. This was definitely an "almost" championship season. Nonetheless Coach Bezdek had fine team and he put together a fine season.

Gettysburg was the first to come to Beaver Stadium for a PSU win W (33-0). The home and season opener was played on October 4. Bucknell was next at New Beaver Stadium for a close match W (9-0). Then came the loss at Dartmouth on October 18.

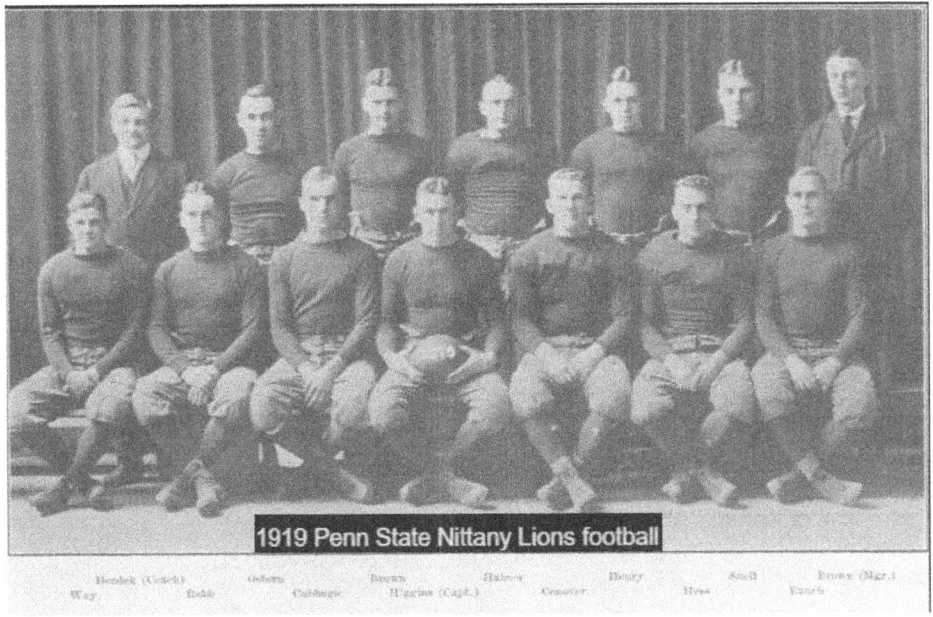

1919 Penn State Nittany Lions football

From here, Ursinas came to visit and were beaten by a toughened Penn State Team W (48-7). The always tough University of Pennsylvania hosted the Nittany Lions and were defeated on November 1 W (10-0). Then on November 8, PSU defeated Lehigh at home W (20-7). PSU took on its third Ivy League school on November 15 at Cornell. The Nittany Lions defeated the Big Red at Schoellkopf Field in Ithaca W (20-0). The annual Thanksgiving trek to Forbes Field to play Pittsburgh was on November 27. PSU prevailed W (20-0).

1920 Penn State Football Season Coach Hugo Bezdek

The 1920 Penn State Nittany Lions football team was coached by Hugo Bezdek. This year the team got seven wins just like 1919, but there were no losses. Penn State was undefeated in 1920 but the season was not perfect. After winning their first seven games to start the season, on November 13, the Nittany Lions played at Lehigh to a tie T (7-7) and the following week on November 25 (Thanksgiving), they tied Pittsburgh T (0-0) at Forbes Field. All the other games were wins. This was an "almost" championship season.

The First five wins were at New Beaver Field: September 25 Muhlenberg W (27-7); then October 2, Gettysburg W (13-0), then

October 9, Dartmouth W (14-7). The following week on October 16, North Carolina State traveled to Beaver Stadium and were beaten W 41-0). Lebanon Valley did not know what hit them in PSU game 5 when the Nittany Lions scored their highest number of points ever W (109-0).

The last two wins were at Penn W (28-7, and Nebraska at home W (20-0). It was on November 6, 1920 that Penn State won its fourth major intersectional game at Beaver Field in its first game against Nebraska, 20-0, on Pennsylvania Day. Glenn Killinger and Charlie Way combine to lead the victory as each scores a touchdown and Killinger passes for another.

Following these two wins came the two ties T (7-7) at Lehigh, and T (0-0) at Pitt.

1921 Penn State Football Season Coach Hugo Bezdek

The 1921 Penn State Nittany Lions football team was coached by Hugo Bezdek in his fourth year. Penn State and Coach Bezdek had another great undefeated season with two ties again. This time, the team garnered eight wins and the first tie was against Harvard on October 20 T (20-20). The second tie was against Pitt on Thanksgiving. Two seasons in a row, neither Penn State nor Pitt scored a point on Thanksgiving Day T (0-0). The first four wins before the Harvard tie were all at home in New Beaver Field. Again, this was a great "almost" championship season.

On September 24, Lebanon Valley came to town and played twice better on defense than the prior year W (53-0. PSU shut out Gettysburg on October 1, W (24-0) Gettysburg scored 24. PSU also shut out North Carolina State one week later W (35-0). The fourth win came from Lehigh on October 28 (28-7). This was followed by the tie T (20-20) at Harvard.

On October 29, The Nittany Lions traveled to the Polo Grounds where the NY Baseball Giants played to take on Georgia Tech W (28-7). Carnegie tech was next at home and the score was the same W (28-7). PSU traveled to Franklin Field to play Navy and won W (13-7) against the Middies. November 24 was Thanksgiving and the annual Pittsburgh excursion to Forbes Field was another tie. In a late

Chapter 13 PSU Football – The Hugo Bezdek Era   75

season game on December 3, he Nittany Lions traveled to the West Coast to play the Washington Huskies and won the game W (21-7)

1922 Penn State Football Season Coach Hugo Bezdek

The 1922 Penn State Nittany Lions football team was coached by Hugo Bezdek. At 6-4-1, PSU opponents got to rejoice this year because, after two unbeaten seasons in a row, and five straight wins in 1922, it appeared nobody was ever going to be able to defeat Hugo Bezdek again.

Then, the magic ended for 1922 on November 3, Navy neat Penn State in Washington DC L (0-14). PSU rebounded the next week against Carnegie Tech at home (W 10-0). In a really tough match against Penn on November 18, PSU missed out by one point L (6-7) and then in the November 30 game against Pittsburgh in Forbes Field, the Nittany Lions lost a close on L (0-14).

With a 6-3-1 record going into the Bowl season, Penn State was selected to play in the January 1 Rose Bowl against USC. The Trojans prevailed against a tough Nittany Lions team in a close game, giving PSU its first Bowl Game Loss (3-14)

The Rose Bowl – A Write up by Penn State University

A Rose Bowl invitation was always like a national championship.

The first of 46 completed bowl games in Penn State program history dates all the way back to 1923, where the Nittany Lions made their Rose Bowl debut against USC on New Year's Day in what would also be the first ever game at the current Rose Bowl Stadium in the Arroyo Seco area of Pasadena.

The 1922 Penn State football season featured more than just a few firsts, including the debut of the Nittany Lion. Making its first appearance, the Penn State mascot donned an African Lion uniform re-purposed from a Penn State player's production of George Bernard Shaw's "Androcles and The Lion" in the first meeting in program history against Syracuse at New York City's Polo Grounds on Oct. 28, 1922.

Under the direction of fifth-year head coach Hugo Bezdek, the Nittany Lions posted a 5-0 record before the outing against the Orange, entering the matchup averaging 33 points per game before playing to a 0-0 tie against Syracuse.

Next up, Penn State was slated to play Navy in a highly-anticipated outing in Washington, D.C. Having not surrendered a loss in 30 consecutive games, Penn State traveled to American League Park to square off against Navy on Nov. 2, 1922. Entering the matchup with a depleted roster due to injuries, the Nittany Lions played in front of a crowd of 35,000 featuring congressmen and dignitaries as well Pittsburgh head coach Pop Warner and Penn's John Heisman. Navy jumped out to a 7-0 lead by halftime before a fake punt and fumble recovery sent the Midshipmen ahead 14-0, with the Nittany Lions ultimately falling short to give Penn State its first loss in 30 games.

Penn State responded with a 10-0 win against Carnegie Tech the following week, but lost back-to-back games at Penn and at Pittsburgh in the yearly Thanksgiving week game to close the regular season.

At 6-3-1, Penn State was set to match up against a University of Southern California squad that had won all but one game on the year, including each of its last four straight for a 9-1-0 record. USC also was making its first overall bowl and Rose Bowl Game appearance against Penn State after Pacific Coast Conference champion California declined the invitation to play in Pasadena. The Trojans' only loss in 1922 had come to the Golden Bears.

Although the trip to the Rose Bowl Game was the first bowl in program history for the Nittany Lions, Bezdek had previously guided Oregon to a victory over Penn in the 1917 Rose Bowl as the Ducks' head coach.

Penn State boarded a train on Dec. 19, making stops in Chicago and the Grand Canyon before arriving in Pasadena on Christmas Eve.

On the day of the game, the Nittany Lions made an appearance at the Tournament of Roses Parade before boarding taxis to head to the game, without a police escort. Los Angeles post-parade traffic created a crisis for the team as the cabs carrying the 29-person travel party navigated through the lawns of local residents before arriving to find that kickoff had been pushed back 10 minutes.

After a bit of contentious discussion between Bezdek and USC head coach Elmer "Gloomy Gus" Henderson, the game was delayed an hour and the game would end under just the light of the moon in the night sky.

Penn State struck first, when quarterback and kicker Myron "Mike" Palm nailed a 20-yard field goal to give the Nittany Lions a 3-0 lead at the end of the first quarter. USC answered with a pair of one-yard touchdown runs in the second and third quarter, respectively to pull ahead 14-3. Neither team would score again as Penn State's defense held off the Trojans in the final frame, but the Nittany Lions couldn't get on the scoreboard again, held to just five first downs in front of the crowd of 43,000.

As the final whistle blew late into the evening, sportswriters had to strike matches to provide enough light to finish filing their stories. Penn State finished the 1922 season at 6-4-1, while also donating its $21,349.64 in Rose Bowl Game profit to the $2 million Emergency Building Fund, directed to the construction of Irvin Hall, which was formerly Varsity Hall.

Since their first meeting in the 1923 Rose Bowl, Penn State and USC have met in two more post-season contests, with the Nittany Lions winning in the 1982 Fiesta Bowl and the Trojans winning in the 2009 Rose Bowl.

Penn State and USC have emerged as two of the nation's most successful programs in bowl success, with the Trojans ranking No. 1 (66.0, 33-17) and the Nittany Lions No. 3 (63.0, 28-16-2) in bowl winning percentage among teams with at least 20 post-season appearances.

End pf PSU write-up on 1922-1923 Rose Bowl.

1923 Penn State Football Season Coach Hugo Bezdek

The 1923 Penn State Nittany Lions football team was coached by Hugo Bezdek for the sixth year. The team looked better than its last year as it posted a 6-2-1 record for the season. Penn State won as many games, tied as many games, played two less games and lost two less games than the prior year. There was no Rose Bowl invitation this year, though the overall record was better.

PSU got an October 27 ticket to Yankee Stadium to play West Virginia and the game ended in a tie T (13-13).

1924 Penn State Football Season Coach Hugo Bezdek

The 1924 Penn State Nittany Lions football team was coached by Hugo Bezdek in his seventh season. He and the team performed very well again with just one more loss and one extra game from the 1923 season. 6-3-1.

1925 Penn State Football Season Coach Hugo Bezdek

The 1925 Penn State Nittany Lions football team was coached by Hugo Bezdek in his eighth season. Though the roaring twenties were at the height of their roaring, the Nittany Lions with a 4-4-1 record clearly had not out-roared as many teams as it had in the recent past.

PSU's Mike Michalske, was one of the "Great Ones."

"Mike" Michalske's illustrious career as a football player began at Penn State, where he was an All-American. All that I could find on his suggests he was a great football player and he is on the list of the 11 best players in PSU history.

After graduating in 1926, he joined the New York Yankees of the American Football League (yes, there was once a Yankees football team!). The Football Yankees joined the National Football League in 1927. In 1929 Michalske joined the Green Bay Packers, who were then coached by "Curly" Lambeau, where he played at guard position during the Packers' championship seasons of 1929 - 1931. At the end of the 1937 season, Mike retired from professional play. As an aside, now you know the origin of the name Lambeau Field.

Mike went on to coach at St. Norbert College, The Lafayette School for Boys, Iowa State University, Baylor University, Texas A&M University, and The University of Texas.

In 1963, Mike was inducted into the Green Bay Packers' Hall of Fame. In 1964, its second year, he was the first guard inducted into the NFL Hall of Fame. He was also inducted into the Wisconsin Athletic Hall of Fame, and was honored with the Red Smith Award. Not too shabby for an offensive lineman.

1926 Penn State Football Season Coach Hugo Bezdek

The 1926 Penn State Nittany Lions football team was coached by Hugo Bezdek. No coach delivers great seasons every year but this season at 5-4 was just a bit better than the last one 4-4-1 for Penn State. PSU settled for no ties in 1926. No championships either.

1927 Penn State Football Season Coach Hugo Bezdek

The 1927 Penn State Nittany Lions football team was coached by Hugo Bezdek to a 6-2-1 record which surely made it seem that PSU was moving again from the prior year's 5-4.

1928 Penn State Football Season Coach Hugo Bezdek

The 1928 Penn State Nittany Lions football team was coached by Hugo Bezdek in his eleventh year with the team. It was a tough year with tough games and PSU did not measure well under the circumstances of the season. The University more or less had had it with football and sports and felt it needed to concentrate on academics instead of sports. The lack of university support crushed the team's opportunities.

At the time, Penn State had decided and in fact, it was downgrading its entire athletic program. There had been nationwide criticism of colleges because some who cared little about sports believed that they had emphasized sports to the detriment of academics. In this year of 1928, Penn State made a bad situation even worse. The school eliminated all new athletic scholarships, and football went into an immediate decline. What had been one of the best teams in the country in the early and mid-1920s became one of the worst of the 1930s. Thank yous to the bean counters with the green eye shades.

Hugo Bezdek was a great coach, regardless but he was not a magician. Looks like our next eight years won't have much good news other than that the program survived. Amen!

This year Bezdek took what he had and out of those players magically created a 6-3 season. That's how good he was. He saw the handwriting and bailed right after 1929, the last smile for awhile.

1929 Penn State Football Season Coach Hugo Bezdek

The 1929 Penn State Nittany Lions football team was coached by Hugo Bezdek in his 12th season. His career paralleled Knute Rockne's but he got another position as Penn State as Director of Athletics in 1930 and did not put in a 13th year as Rockne had. The team was 6-3 this year in Hugo's last season. There would be nothing close to championship years after this until Higgins 1937 season so we won't be showing much for about 8 more seasons.

Rockne got hit with the same crap at Notre Dame. The Administration wanted Einsteins instead of Joe Montana's. The difference, however was that neither Bezdek nor his successor Bob Higgins had the *schmooze factor* as Rockne had to help his players get free rides to PSU.

This, 1929, would be Bezdek's finest season since the slide and it would be the best that PSU could muster for the next nine years. The PSU scholarship plan for athletes had kicked in and it was surprising to many that this year's 6-3 season was as positive as it was for the Nittany Lions.

Chapter 14 Bob Higgins Era 1930-1949

Coach # 11 Bob Higgins
Coach # 12 Joe Bedenk

1930	Bob Higgins	3-4-2	Coach # 11
1931	Bob Higgins	2-8	
1932	Bob Higgins	2-5	
1933	Bob Higgins	3-3-1	
1934	Bob Higgins	4-4	
1935	Bob Higgins	4-4	
1936	Bob Higgins	3-5	
1937	Bob Higgins	5-3	
1938	Bob Higgins	3-4-1	
1939	Bob Higgins	5-1-2	
1940	Bob Higgins	6-1-1	
1941	Bob Higgins	7-2	
1942	Bob Higgins	6-1-1	
1943	Bob Higgins	5-3-1	
1944	Bob Higgins	6-3	
1945	Bob Higgins	5-3	
1946	Bob Higgins	6-2	
1947	Bob Higgins	9-0-1	
1948	Bob Higgins	7-1-1	
1949	Joe Bedenk	5-4	Coach # 12

You can see from this record until 1937 that if it were not the administration's "no athletic scholarship's" fault, Bob Higgins would have been fired before 1936. He endured and Higgins should have been getting "combat" pay for working without armaments (players).

PSU 1930 Football Team – Coach Higgins is not present

1930 Penn State Football Season Coach Bob Higgins

The 1930 Penn State Nittany Lions football team was coached by Bob Higgins in his first year as Penn State's head coach.

Bob Higgins was born Nov. 24, 1893. He was a native of Corning, N.Y. He came to Penn State as a student in 1914 and soon became one of the best players of all time. He was an All-American Selection in 1915 and 1919 and his talents helped him get selected into the College Football Hall of Fame in 1954.

Bob Higgins

Higgins was one of only five players in the history of Nittany Lion football to earn five letters. He served as captain of the team as a senior when he was named to the 1919 Walter Camp All-American team.

Higgins was a multi-faceted athlete who also lettered in baseball, boxing and wrestling. After College, he played two years of professional football with the Canton Bulldogs.

His coaching career before Penn State included stays at West Virginia Wesleyan and Washington University in St. Louis, before he returned to Penn State in 1928 as an assistant.

Bob Higgins was appointed the Lions' head coach in 1930. Eventually, he got through the scholarship reduction period that lasted until 1938-1940, and he compiled a very respectable 91-57-11 record in 19 seasons—the most ever seasons for any PSU coach at the time.

We'll cover his great 1947 team in this chapter. It was unbeaten in the regular-season and tied Southern Methodist, 13-13, in the 1948 Cotton Bowl. Higgins, who died in 1969, received many honors as a player and as a coach. For example, he is a college hall-of-famer and he was selected by the International News Service (precursor to UPI) in 1915 and Walter Camp in 1919. His 85-yard touchdown reception against Pittsburgh was immortalized in Knute Rockne's "Great Football Plays."

1931 Penn State Football Season Coach Bob Higgins

The 1931 Penn State Nittany Lions football team was coached by Bob Higgins in his second year at the helm. Penn State was in year two of its eight game slump (2-8 this year) due to scholarship restrictions. Bob Higgins team struggled for just two wins in ten games this year. With good players at a premium, the Nittany Lions had a tough time beating anybody.

1932 Penn State Football Season Coach Bob Higgins

The 1932 Penn State Nittany Lions football team was coached by Bob Higgins in his third year. For whatever reasons after the dismal 1931 season, Penn State scheduled only seven games and recorded a 2-5 season for 1932.

1933 Penn State Football Season Coach Bob Higgins

The 1933 Penn State Nittany Lions football team was coached by Bob Higgins. The team improved somewhat to a .500 record at 3-3 with a tie. For some reason, more teams seemed to be paring down their schedules to seven games and focusing on intramural sports for all students.

1934 Penn State Football Season Coach Bob Higgins

The 1934 Penn State Nittany Lions football team was coached by Bob Higgins. In 1934, Higgins' PSU team had a so year at 4-4. The team played one more game than in the last two years. The country seemed to be getting over (not 100%) its predisposition at the time in these depression years that playing sports at the collegiate level was bad.

Since not all teams shut down their athletic scholarships, typical powerhouses such as Penn State were overwhelmed by alumni and friends who were bugging the administration to make life better for the team.

Eventually the coach right after Bob Higgins, Joe Bedenk, would benefit as Penn State adapted to the needs of athletics and academics. Somehow it was forgotten that the lucky sports people who received scholarships for their athleticism also got an opportunity to compete in the real world with a college degree from a great institution, Penn State,

Seasons had begun to start later and this year, 1934, the date was October 6 at home and the opponent was Lebanon Valley who had muscled up and had become a real football team. Penn State beat them in a tough game W (13-0).

1935 Penn State Football Season Coach Bob Higgins

The 1935 Penn State Nittany Lions football team was coached by Bob Higgins in his sixth year at Penn State. His 1935 record was 4-4, which was a theoretical mirror image of the final record of 1934. Higgins worked with what he had and a *give-up* coach might not have done so well with all walk-ons. Bob Higgins taught a lot of great kids how to play great football because he had to and because he wanted to. Nobody with God's best talent was knocking on the door of Penn State at the time because it was an institution that made them pay tuition to play for the university.

1936 Penn State Football Season Coach Bob Higgins

The 1936 Penn State Nittany Lions football team was coached by Bob Higgins in his seventh year. Times were tough for PSU as the walk-ons were not about to bring the University national championships or even braggable seasons. The 3-5 1936 season was another of the lollygaggers that only PSU lovers at the time cared about. Academicians were quite pleased as athletics had been minimized so well by the administration that PSU had taken itself out of the national picture for the seventh year.

A lot of brave hearts came forth and got to play football at a great university. However, with PSU saying no and choosing not to offer degrees to all of the exceptional athletes in America who were graduating as great football athletes, the university and the team suffered, there were few of America's exceptional teammates who had the tuition in their pocket when great universities were offering them a free ride, who came to Penn State. Thus, there were very few if any recognized great athletes from whom these great and powerful scrappy PSU walk-ons could learn the full knack of the game. Just a few scholarship athletes would have helped in many ways.

1937 Penn State Football Season Coach Bob Higgins

The 1937 Penn State Nittany Lions football team coached by Bob Higgins in his eighth season. Many college programs would have dumped Higgins as an inadequate coach because of his record to this point. Give PSU credit for keeping one of its greatest coaches of all time on the sidelines with his team as the university was sorting out whether it wanted to win football games or not.

Without a great coach such as Bob Higgins, who knows how well all-walk-on teams would have performed against the talented teams AD Hugo Bezdek had scheduled for them to play. In a nutshell, the word is "Bravo" to coach Higgins for keeping PSU football respectable while it was wondering if it needed to survive at all.

This season Higgins team broke out of the funk from the last eight years and posted a winning record (5-3). This would not be the last PSU winning record as all college teams began to offer scholarships again to deserving athletes again and the academicians seemed OK with the university having a winning record in college sports.

Bob Higgins' Nittany Lions finished their first winning season in seven years 5-3, and nobody was complaining.

1938 Penn State Football Season Coach Bob Higgins

The 1938 Penn State Nittany Lions football team was coached by Bob Higgins in his ninth year. Though the Scholarship ban was mitigated, the teams were not ready to be formed based on a poor track record. So, Higgins had a tough 1938 season. Think about with all the losses he sustained in PSU's dark seasons how bright it will be as we move forward through the rest of Bob Higgins's seasons as he captured the hearts and mind so Americans what loved PSU football. Not this year's 3-4-1 season. No championship there folks.

1939 Penn State Football Season Coach Bob Higgins

The 1939 Penn State Nittany Lions football team rebounded this year to 5-1-2 after some poor years. The team was coached by Bob Higgins in his tenth year. The apparent doom and gloom of the *walk-on era* had finally faded and the Penn State administration had finally permitted Coach Higgins to invite scholarship athletes to the campus as many other Division I type teams had been doing since 1928, when PSU imposed its own ban.

Penn State played eight games and had just one loss, which was a shutout blowout against Cornell in the third game of the season on October 14 in Ithaca, NY. L (0-47). The ties were in the middle of the season and near the end of the season. The first was at Syracuse T (6-6) on October 28, and the second was at Army T (14-14) in Michie Stadium, West Point, NY. This was a championship caliber team.

The Nittany Lions opened the season with two wins at New Beaver Field. The first game on October 7, was against Bucknell which had been playing tough football over the past several years W (13-3). The next home game was against Lehigh on October 4 and the Lions came through with a big win W (49-7). The next week was the loss at Cornell followed by the Syracuse tie and then another home game on November 4 v Maryland W (12-0).

Penn State knew that it had recovered when on November 11, it beat Penn at Penn W (10-0). The Army tie was next followed by what in years' past would have been a Thanksgiving Day game against Pitt. New Beaver Field was the site of the game on November 25, and PSU had gotten so good that the once hard to ever beat Pitt Panthers lost W (10-0)

In this game, future All-American Leon Gajecki led Penn State to its first victory over Pitt in 20 years in this 10-0 upset before a record-tying crowd of 20,000 at Beaver Field. Penn State finishes the year with its best record since 1921 at 5-1-2. It's amazing what a little funding for football will do.

1939 Thanksgiving Story

Here is a little known fact: In 1939, President Franklin Delano Roosevelt declared November 23rd, the next-to-last Thursday of the month, to be Thanksgiving Day. This break with tradition was prompted by requests from the National Retail Dry Goods Association to extend the Christmas shopping season by one week.

I was wondering as I wrote about so many PSU v Pitt games prior to this year, as to why Thanksgiving always seemed to be on the last Thursday during this period. The above answers that question for me but then again, why not Friday?

I know this is not a football story but it is a neat story anyway and it did affect the annual PSU Pitt game so we include it here simply because it is quite interesting.

In 1929, F.B. Havilland asked president Hoover to move Thanksgiving to Friday? Obviously, Hoover said: "No!" Havilland hoped that American workers could get a nice three-day weekend. It did not happen. But, why not?

Did you ever wonder why we carve our succulent gobblers on the fourth Thursday of November? It clearly is not because Thanksgiving Thursday sounds better than Thanksgiving Friday.

The Thanksgiving idea as we all know happened with the Pilgrims. In 1789, President Washington declared that Thursday, Nov. 26, would be a "Day of Public Thanksgiving," according to the National Archives. It became more or less, a holiday to celebrate. But subsequent to 1789, the date for the holiday was announced by a yearly presidential proclamation.

It was thus celebrated on various days and months. None of us were living then and American football had yet to be invented, so even our grandparents do not remember the notion of a floating Thanksgiving holiday.

When President Lincoln made his Thanksgiving proclamation in 1863, the last Thursday of November became the standard.

In 1939, there was a big dispute over the date. Two Thanksgiving holidays were observed as the dispute was so large. People were outraged that the holiday was changed by the President just so the people would spend more money.

According to the Franklin D. Roosevelt Presidential Library and Museum, a five-Thursday November fell in 1933 and some retailers asked President Roosevelt to move the holiday up a week so there would be an extra week of shopping and it would help the retail trade. The president denied the request and Americans ate their turkey on the last Thursday as always in 1933.

But, as we know, Roosevelt was president for a long time, and it was plenty long enough for a change of heart when he got another request from merchants. The dispute lasted two years. A few governors decided their states would have Thanksgiving on the last Thursday of the month as usual and that's how some people ended up celebrating it a week earlier or later than others. Pass the gravy.

1940 Penn State Football Season Coach Bob Higgins

The 1940 Penn State Nittany Lions football team was coached by Bob Higgins. The team played eight games again and had a nice 6-1-1 record. As usual, home games were played in New Beaver Field in University Park, Pennsylvania. No championship—not enough games.

The only loss of the season was the last game on November 23, against an always tough Pittsburgh Panther team at Pitt Stadium L (7-20).

1941 Penn State Football Season Coach Bob Higgins

The 1941 Penn State Nittany Lions football team was coached by Bob Higgins in his twelfth year as head coach. PSU was on a comeback roll and this year, they were also increasing the game son the schedule to 9 from 8. This 7-2 season was a great season for Bob Higgins and the Penn State Nittany Lions. But, no championships or "almosts."

In researching all about Bob Higgins, I was so glad to hear about the scholarship problem being in Higgins early years because his overall record is so good, these years, such as 1941 are the make-up years that are part of getting that great record of Higgins, great! Unlike fiction, in this book we've got some great reading ahead as Higgins is coach for eight more years and he has a lot of wins to amass.

This year, though here were nine games, the season began in October, on the 4th, my wedding anniversary. It was not a good season opener as the Nittany Lions had traveled to Civic Stadium in Buffalo NY, lots of miles from Colgate's Hamilton campus, and were defeated in a clawing match by the Red Raiders L (0-7).

On October 11, Bucknell, a recent tough team came to New Beaver Field and gave it up to Penn State W (27-13) in a tough match. Temple, a great academic institution had become a tough team in the 1930's and had a lot of moxie when the Nittany Lions came to their stadium on October 18 and were beaten in a close battle L (0-14).

In 1941, that was the end of the losses. Lehigh visited New Beaver Field and were defeated on October 25 W (40-6). Penn State then traveled to the Polo Grounds on a rare Friday game on October 31. At the same exact date, Mount Rushmore was completed. The opponent for PSU was New York University and the Lions disposed of this team in a shut-out W (42-0).

An always tough # 18 ranked Syracuse team came to Penn State on November 8, to play a game of football at New Beaver Field in what had become a rivalry match. Penn State took all the marbles this day against the Orangemen in a great win W (34-19). West Virginia's defense held PSU to 7 points on November 15 while PSU shut-out the Mountaineers at home W (7-0).

Always expecting a tough game, PSU traveled to Pitt Stadium to take on the Panthers and beat them good in this long-time rivalry W (31-7). Finishing up the season just a little later than normal, PSU played South Carolina at Carolina Stadium W (19–12) for fine 7-2 season for Higgins. Soon Coach Higgins would be getting national recognition for the Penn State Nittany Lions.

1942 Penn State Football Season Coach Bob Higgins

The 1942 Penn State Nittany Lions football team was coached by Bob Higgins in his thirteenth season. There was no bad luck, PSU played eight games and somehow kept missing undefeated by one game 6-1-1. After doing well consistently for the last several years before 1942, PSU had gained respect again as a national powerhouse for football. Penn was the only ranked team that Penn State played this year. This year, 1942, the team was ranked at # 19 by the AP.

1943 Penn State Football Season Coach Bob Higgins

The 1943 Penn State Nittany Lions football team was coached by Bob Higgins in his fourteenth year. All college football teams with good coaches or great coaches need great players to be great. Good and great coaches such as Bob Higgins do the best they can with what they get and every now and then, things happen on the field that make the season better or worse than it should have been.

After a 6-1-1 season in 1943 and a # 19 finish in the AP poll, PSU had one less win and two more losses than in 1942. So, there was no ranking and no bowl games but the team had done did fine. Pundits might suggest that this year, Higgins team suffered a 5-3-1 season but in such a successful season there was little suffering. It is always nice to win every game but sometimes this cannot be done because of many different circumstances.

1944 Penn State Football Season Coach Bob Higgins

The 1944 Penn State Nittany Lions football team was coached by Bob Higgins in his fifteenth season. Higgins was a great coach and played this year to a 6-3, nine game season.

1945 Penn State Football Season Coach Bob Higgins

The 1945 Penn State Nittany Lions football team was coached by Bob Higgins in his sixteenth season with the team. The team played just eight games and had a very respectable record of 5-3.

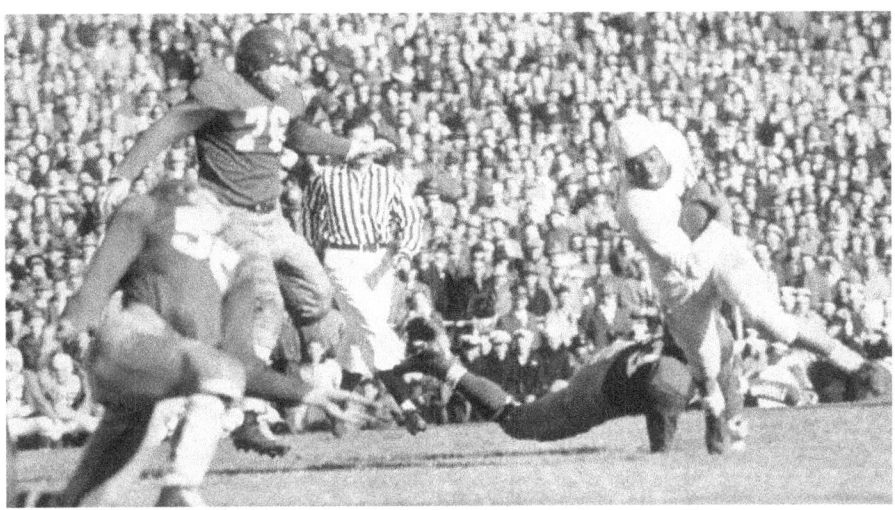

Freshman tailback Wally Triplett was Penn State's first African-American player to start a game (Michigan State, 1945) and was instrumental in the Nittany Lions compiling a 23-3-2 record from 1946-48.

1946 Penn State Football Season Coach Bob Higgins

Guard Steve Suhey earned first-team All-America honors in 1947 and was a member of arguably the most prominent family in Penn State football history. Suhey married a daughter, Ginger, of Penn State All-American and future head coach, Bob Higgins, and three of their sons — Paul, Larry and Matt Suhey — played for Penn State in the 1970s. Kevin and Joe Suhey became fourth-generation members of the Higgins-Suhey family to play for the Nittany Lions during the 2000s.

The 1946 Penn State Nittany Lions football team was coached by Bob Higgins in his seventeenth season as coach. There still was no Beaver Stadium and so Higgins and the great PSU teams of his year played their games at the New Beaver Field in University Park, Pennsylvania. As time went on, New Beaver Field would not be enough to hold the crowds but that day had yet to come.

The 1947 Penn State Nittany Lions football team was coached by Bob Higgins in his eighteenth season. The team was 9-0 in the regular season, which might have been good enough for national championship but in the bowl game, the best they could do was tie. PSU had its best season under Higgins, undefeated in regular season with a tie in the bowl game. Bravo PSU and Bravo Bob Higgins for a # 4 consensus finish in 1947.

Nobody beat Penn State throughout the whole season so let me just repeat the scores. They are all wins for PSU. We all knew Higgins had it in him from watching him from 1928 and finally in 1947, he produced a superior team. This time, however, his boys made national news.

On September 20, in a game played at Hershey Park Stadium in Hershey, PA PSU defeated Washington State W (27-40> Then, on Oct. 4, at home, PSU played Bucknell W (54-0).

1947 Penn State Football Season Coach Bob Higgins

On January 1, 1948, just a few days from my birthday (I mean my birth-date when I first began to breathe) PSU and SMU battled hard to come up with the best they could, a tie T (13-13). The Cotton Bowl Classic, before the days of the tie breakers, ended in 1947 in a tie game. Bravo to both teams. Higgins coached PSU finished # 4 in the final season rankings. Maybe OK; Maybe not!

Wallace Triplett, Maurice Hoogard Cotton Bowl

The January 1, 1948 was the last bowl game Penn State played before Joe Paterno was on its coaching staff. It was a historic moment in college football for another reason. It was amid the backdrop of segregation in Texas that two Nittany Lions became the first black players to compete in the Cotton Bowl at Dallas Stadium.

Wallace Triplett and Dennie Hoggard helped Penn State gain a comeback 13-13 tie against Southern Methodist that marked the first time a team with African-American players competed in Texas against a team from a segregated university.

The story of Mr. Triplett for sure is truly inspiring. For Triplett, now 90, (April 21) the 1948 Cotton Bowl was among the first benchmarks of his historic career. He became the first African-American to start a football game for Penn State. He also became the first black player to be drafted by, and play for, a National Football League team in 1949.

Wallace Triplett played four seasons in the NFL, two with the Detroit Lions. There he was a teammate of Doak Walker, SMU's all-America tailback against whom Triplett competed in Dallas. The 1948 Cotton Bowl ended in a tie after the late Hoggard nearly caught the game-winning pass on the final play.

"Doak used to tell me, 'Wally, the best thing about that game was that there was no winner,'" Triplett said. "And I agreed with him." The 1947 # 4 team was one of Penn State's best, finishing the regular season 9-0, and outscoring opponents 319-27. The high-scoring offense featured Triplett at wingback and Pen Argyl's Elwood Petchel at tailback.

Penn State's postseason plans stalled, however, because head coach Bob Higgins would not accept an invitation from a bowl that wouldn't allow Triplett and Hoggard to attend. In 1946, Penn State players voted not to play a scheduled game at the University of Miami, which had the same policy. A year later the players decided there would be no vote.

"[All-America lineman] Steve Suhey said, 'We're Penn State, there will be no meetings,'" Triplett said. "And that was it."

(Suhey's comment is said to have precipitated the "We are Penn State" chant, but Penn State football historian Lou Prato has traced the cheer's origin to the 1970s).

1948: Penn State, with running back Wally Triplett (pictured, right) and end Dennie Hoggard, plays SMU in the Cotton

Southern Methodist, meanwhile, was 9-0-1 and ranked No. 3 after winning the Southwest Conference and wanted to face the best opponent possible in the Cotton Bowl. To coach Matty Bell, that was No. 4 Penn State.

Penn State's appearance in the 1948 Cotton Bowl was significant on several fronts. Wally Triplett and end Dennie Hoggard became the first African-Americans to play in the Cotton Bowl game and helped Penn State to a 9-0-1 record in 1947, with the only blemish a 13-13 tie with Southern Methodist in the Cotton Bowl. Behind a defense that posted six shutouts, Penn State won its first Lambert Trophy and its No. 4 final ranking was its highest in program history to date.

The game itself was a classic in Cotton Bowl history. Petchel rallied Penn State from a 13-0 deficit by throwing two touchdown passes, one to Triplett in the third quarter.

On the final play, Petchel threw a pass in the end zone intended for Hoggard, though Triplett was nearby as well. An SMU player deflected the pass, which floated toward Hoggard

1948 Penn State Football Season Coach Bob Higgins

The 1948 Penn State Nittany Lions football team was coached by Bob Higgins in his 19th and last season. After an undefeated regular season in 1947, it was tough to equal such a performance but Higgins came close with a 7-1-1 record. He was a great coach and in many ways put PSU back on the map. He never had the benefit of a scholarship team. Championships were in Higgins blood.

This was his last year of a great tenure.

1949 Penn State Football Season Coach Joe Bedenk

The 1949 Penn State Nittany Lions football team was coached by Joe Bedenk. Bob Higgins had coached at Penn State for nineteen years and had an enviable record of 91–57–11 after having gone through the walk-on years. Think about how well he did when freed from the shackles. He is a coach of many enviable talents. However this year, the team record was just 5-4.

Bedenk was named head coach after he had coached the offensive line for several years. After this single 5–4 season, Coach Bedenk requested a return to coaching the offensive line, and Penn State brought in Rip Engle as head coach in 1950. From thence, PSU's modern history began and eventually, I too would be "listening to" and then watching Penn State games.

In September, the first class of scholarship players since 1927 entered Penn State but were sent to California State Teachers College to reside because of crowded housing conditions on the main campus. Among the freshmen were future starters Joe Yukica, Don Barney, Jim Dooley and Joe Gratson. The talent drought was over.

September 24 PSU kicked off its season with a kick in the pants on a L (6-27) to Villanova at home, Things did not get better as a tough Army team beat PSU by a wide margin L (7-42) at Michie Stadium in West Point, NY. The Nittany Lions took on Boston College, new to the schedule on October 8 and picked up their first win of the season and first win for Coach Joe Bedenk W (32-14). Nebraska came to New Beaver Field on October 15 and PSU won that encounter W (22-7).

A tough Michigan State team hosted the Nittany Lions on October 22 and beat PSU in a shutout at Spartan Stadium L (0-24. Penn State would win its next three games under Joe Bedenk until Pittsburgh delivered a loss to the Nittany Lions on November 19 in the season closer L (0-19). On October 29, Syracuse traveled to New Beaver Field to take on the Nittany Lions and PSU won the game W (33-21).

On November 5, the Lions traveled to West Virginia and beat the Mountaineers at Mountaineer Field in Morgantown W (34-14). PSU traveled on November 14 to defeat Temple at Temple Stadium W (28-7). Coach Bedenk finished the season at 5-4.

Chapter 15 Rip Engle Era 1950-1965

Rip Engle Coach # 13

Year	Coach	Record
1950	Rip Engle	5-3-1
1951	Rip Engle	5-4
1952	Rip Engle	7-2-1
1953	Rip Engle	6-3
1954	Rip Engle	7-2-
1955	Rip Engle	5-4
1956	Rip Engle	6-2-1
1957	Rip Engle	6-3
1958	Rip Engle	6-3-1
1959	Rip Engle	9-2
1960	Rip Engle	7-3
1961	Rip Engle	8-3
1962	Rip Engle	9-2
1963	Rip Engle	7-3
1964	Rip Engle	6-4
1965	Rip Engle	5-5

Top row, left to right: Dan Radakovich, Joe McMullen, George Welsh, Joe Paterno, J.T. White Bottom row, left to right: Frank Patrick, Earl Bruce, Rip Engle, Jim O'Hora taken during the football Field Day in 1963

On April 22, 1950 Charles A. "Rip" Engle, who had been head coach at Brown University was named the new Penn State head football coach to replace Joe Bedenk.

Engle was the innovator of the famous Wing-T formation. His teams experienced tremendous success leading Engle to a career PSU record of 104-48-4.

In May of 1950 Engle named former Brown University quarterback Joseph V. Paterno to his Penn State staff. He promptly assigned Paterno to coach quarterbacks. Rip Engle coached his last game in 1965 with a win over Maryland, 19-7 ending a 16-year stint as Penn State head football coach. This Paterno guy had done so well as an assistant that good things were offered him.

During Engle's tenure, Penn State did not endure a losing season. Engle officially retired February 18, 1966. A day later Joseph V. Paterno was hired head football coach of Pennsylvania State University. The rest, as they say, is history. Make sure your history books are not biased. Paterno was a good man and a great coach. .

1950 Penn State Football Season Coach Rip Engle

The 1950 Penn State Nittany Lions football team was coached by Rip Engle in his first year. Coach Engle compiled a 5-3-1 record in his first year with the Nittany Lions. Engle was good but not good enough to make a 5-3-1 effort into a championship season. We will glide through all such great efforts with no championships without shwing all of the games in those particular seasons.

1951 Penn State Football Season Coach Rip Engle

The 1951 Penn State Nittany Lions football team was coached by Rip Engle. The team had a 5-4 record for 1951.

1952 Penn State Football Season Coach Rip Engle

The 1952 Penn State Nittany Lions football team was coached by Rip Engle and played a fine season with a record of 7-2-1. PSU was back to ten games per season. The season began earlier on September 20 at home against Temple W (20-13).

1953 Penn State Football Season Coach Rip Engle

The 1953 Penn State Nittany Lions football team was coached by Rip Engle. They played home games in New Beaver Field in University Park, Pennsylvania. The Field had room for 30,000 fans. This season's record was 6-3 and the team played nine games.

1954 Penn State Football Season Coach Rip Engle

The 1954 Penn State Nittany Lions football team was coached by Rip Engle in his fifth year. The team finished with a 7-2 record and achieved a #16 ranking in the coaches' poll and a #20 in the AP.

1955 Penn State Football Season Coach Rip Engle

The 1955 Penn State Nittany Lions football team was coached by Rip Engle. The team talent pendulum swings and changes from year to year as one team is better than another and vice versa. This year's team made it above .500 with a 5-4 record but otherwise, it was not a stellar year. Rip Engle had better years as you will see. He coached the Lions until 1965.

Lenny Moore was a PSU Great 1955

Leonard Edward Moore was born November 25, 1933. He played halfback at PSU and he played pro for the NFL Baltimore Colts from 1956 to 1967. Moore was simply great. He was NFL Rookie of the Year in 1956 and was a Pro-Bowler seven times. He was inducted into the Pro Football Hall of Fame in 1975.

Moore could to it all and Joe Paterno had him do it all just as Moore did for his great college and pro football career. He was both a great runner and receiver. He would line up both in the backfield as a halfback and split wide as a flanker, and the talented Moore was equally dangerous at both positions

Lenny Moore was among the greatest players to wear the blue and white. In 1954, he became the first Nittany Lion to rush for more than 1,000 yards in a season, gaining 1,082 with 11 touchdowns. Moore was a dynamic runner, receiver and kick returner, accumulating 3,543 all-purpose yards from 1953-55. Moore was selected by the Baltimore Colts in the first round of the 1956 NFL Draft and had a brilliant 12-year career with the Colts, playing in seven Pro Bowls and gaining induction into the Pro Football Hall of Fame in 1975.

His QB at Baltimore was the great Johnny Unitas. To play so many years in the NFL you have got to be pretty darned good and pretty darned tough.

Moore averaged at least 7.0 yards a carry in several seasons. He pulled in 40 receptions for 687 yards and seven touchdowns in 1957, the first of five straight years in which he would have 40 or more catches. In 1958, he caught a career-high of 50 passes for 938 yards and seven touchdowns. This year, he helped the Colts win the NFL championship. Then in 1959, Moore had 47 receptions for 846 yards and six TDs as the Colts repeated as champions.

Leonard Edward Moore is a football player that I have been hearing about forever or so it seems from when I was a little tyke. I remember Lenny playing with Johnny Unitas and the Baltimore Colts but I do not remember well if at all at Penn State and that surely may be my fault. In my defense, I was just seven years old and we did not have a TV until I was 8. Upon making the transition from PSU to the Colts, Moore was immediately great as a pro and had a fantastically productive first pro season.

As noted above, he was named the NFL Rookie of the Year. Here is a pic from 2009 with JoePa at the Syracuse game. Joe Paterno was Assistant Coach when Lenny played in 1955. You can see just by looking at this picture that the two had great admiration for each other.

Chapter 15 The Rip Engle Era   101

Pro football Hall of Famer and former Penn State running back Lenny Moore embraces coach Joe Paterno before the start of the Syracuse game at Beaver Statdium. Moore served as honorary captain for the Lions.

Joe Hermitt (jhermitt@pennlive.com) captured the essence of JoePa and Lanny Moore and their relationship in the above picture. This is from the Syracuse game September 15, 2009. Thank you to Pennlive for the use of the picture and the article to make this book and even more outstanding read for Penn Staters.

1956 Penn State Football Season Coach Rip Engle

The 1956 Penn State (5-4) Nittany Lions football team was coached by Rip Engle in his seventh year as head coach.

1957 Penn State Football Season Coach Rip Engle

The 1957 Penn State Nittany Lions football team was coached by Rip Engle in his eighth season. Engle directed the team to a nice 6-3.

1958 Penn State Football Season Coach Rip Engle

The 1958 Penn State Nittany Lions football team was coached by Rip Engle in his ninth year. Penn State played a tenth game in 1958 and without that game the season would have been 6-3, but with the tie at West Virginia on November 8 T (14-14) the record was 6-3-1.

1959 Penn State Football Season Coach Rip Engle

The 1959 Penn State Nittany Lions football team was coached by Rip Engle in his tenth season of sixteen with PSU. This was the first eight-win year for an Engle team and it brought them a shot at the Liberty Bowl which they won on December 31, 1959 v Alabama W (7-0). The Lions finished at 9-2.

Penn State was winning every game all year until it ran into some old rivals. By now, by reading this book's review of all the games by coach, you know who they are. PSU was 7-0 when it ran into an always stubborn Syracuse team at home. Syracuse was ranked #4 when they played at New Beaver Field. In a brawl, they barely beat Penn State L (18-20) to put the first blemish on Engle's 1959 team. Think about what would have happened if PSU won that game. Syracuse went on to win their first and only National Championship with the help of future Heisman trophy winner Ernie Davis.

In the See-Saw end of season match, looking for every opportunity to have a one-loss season, Pittsburgh spoiled it for the Nittany Lions in a well-fought game L (7-22)

1960 Penn State Football Season Coach Rip Engle

The 1960 Penn State Nittany Lions football team was coached by Rip Engle in his eleventh year. This year the Nittany Lions played their games in the newly opened Beaver Stadium in University Park, Pennsylvania. The team played ten games and finished their first season in their big, brand new stadium with a fine 7-3 record. PSU finished # 16 for the season and if the number of bowl games were as today, PSU would have assured itself of a bowl game match.

The 500-seat Beaver Field, then the 30,000 seat New Beaver Field, and in 1960, the new Beaver stadium were all named for James Beaver, President of the Board of Trustees. The Nittany Lions played at the original Beaver Field and New Beaver Field from when they moved off the lawn until 1959.

The university decided to disassemble the stadium and move it to its current location after the 1959 season. PSU played its first game in the rebuilt stadium on September 17, 1960 against Boston University. Beaver Stadium's horseshoe configuration enabled it to have a seating capacity of 46,284, but as we all know it fits well over 100,000 today after many expansions.

1961 Penn State Football Season Coach Rip Engle

The 1961 Penn State Nittany Lions football team was coached by Rip Engle in his twelfth season. The lions pounded out a #19 finish and a #17 in the AP with an overall season ending 8-3 record including a Gator Bowl win v Georgia Tech.

1962 Penn State Football Season Coach Rip Engle

The 1962 Penn State Nittany Lions football team was coached by Rip Engle in his thirteenth of sixteen seasons. The team was 9-2 with no championships and it played its second set of home games in the brand-new Beaver Stadium in University Park, Pennsylvania.

1963 Penn State Football Season Coach Rip Engle

The 1963 Penn State Nittany Lions football team was coached by Rip Engle in his fourteenth of sixteen seasons. The team played its third set of home games in its brand-new Beaver Stadium in University Park, Pennsylvania. The regular season finale with Pittsburgh was postponed from Nov. 23 to Dec. 7 following the assassination of President John F. Kennedy on Nov. 22 in Dallas, Texas. Even football history cannot undue history, though we wish it could. This year PSU had a 7-3 fine season but no championship.

1964 Penn State Football Season Coach Rip Engle

The 1964 Penn State Nittany Lions football team was coached by Rip Engle in his fifteenth year. Even though the team was just 6-4, its strength of schedule prompted the coach's poll to rank PSU # 14 in 1964.

1965 Penn State Football Season Coach Rip Engle

The 1965 Penn State Nittany Lions football team was coached by Rip Engle's in his last season as head coach of Penn State. Penn State ironically had one of its worst records this year (5-5) as it proves the ups and downs of college football results. Rip Engle was a fine coach. With sixteen seasons of coaching PSU behind him Engle had had enough. He never had a losing season.

Chapter 16 Joe Paterno Era 1966 to 1980

Coach # 14

Year	Coach	Record
1966	Joe Paterno	5-5
1967	Joe Paterno	8-2-1
1968	Joe Paterno	11-0
1969	Joe Paterno	11-0
1970	Joe Paterno	7-3
1971	Joe Paterno	11-1
1972	Joe Paterno	10-2
1973	Joe Paterno	12-0
1974	Joe Paterno	10-2
1975	Joe Paterno	9-3
1976	Joe Paterno	7-5
1977	Joe Paterno	11-1
1978	Joe Paterno	11-1
1979	Joe Paterno	8-4
1980	Joe Paterno	10-2

Coached 45 great seasons 1966 to 2010 and part of 2011.

With 409 victories, Joe Paterno is the winningest coach in NCAA FBS history.

Joe Paterno, defamed by a press out to get him in his waning years, put together bowl victories, two consensus National Championships—1982, 1986, and five undefeated and untied seasons—1968, 1969, 1973, 1986, and 1994. Four of Penn State's unbeaten teams (1968, 1969, 1973, and 1994) won major bowl games and yet were not awarded a national championship. You make the call on that one, please! At the end of the 2011 season, he was the winningest coach ever in Division I with a 409-136-3 record. He was the best coach ever! He was not a good human resources guy but he was a great man who cared about so many people, his archives will be full of plaudits.

1966 Penn State Football Season Coach Joe Paterno

The 1966 Penn State Nittany Lions football team was coached by Joe Paterno in his first season as head coach of Penn State. Paterno helped the team achieve a 5-5 record, which coincidentally was the record for PSU in Rip Engle's last season. No championships, and no almosts. Just an OK year.

September 17 was the First Paterno-led game at home (Beaver Stadium). PSU beat Maryland in a lose match W (15-7).

It is always a good feeling and often a harbinger of good things to come when a new coach wins his first game, especially a home game. Paterno brought in the big one when he was still more or less a kid at 40 years old. Tons of victories later, and Paterno teams would bring in over 400 victories for the good of Penn State University, a great school, and a great football program. September 17th was simply the first. The attendance was almost at max to see this game with 40,911 excited Penn State Fans ready to see the Nittany Lions play ball.

1967 Penn State Football Season Coach Joe Paterno – Gator Bowl Game

The 1967 Penn State Nittany Lions football team was coached by Joe Paterno and played its home games in the recently built Beaver Stadium in University Park, Pennsylvania. It did not take Joe Paterno long to break out of the regular pack of American coaches. Rip Engle and many PSU coaches were very good coaches.

Joe Paterno at 45 years was a remarkable, unquestionably great coach. In his getting to know you first year, he was 5-5 but those days for the most part were gone. In 1967 Paterno showed his mettle and delivered a great 8-2-1 season to PSU fans. Penn State had been a National power. Joe Paterno made Penn State a "you better notice us" national phenomenon. No championship but a great season.

For their great record, the Nittany Lions were invited to the Gator Bowl which was on ABC TV played in Jacksonville Florida against Florida State University on December 30, 1967. It was a really tough game and no team got the edge. This is one bowl game that ended in a tie (T 17-17) before 68,019—all of whom were disappointed.

The Gator Bowl

Penn State was ranked tenth in the nation. FSU entered the Gator Bowl as the underdog. The Nittany Lions had already been awarded the Lambert Trophy as the best team in the eastern United States. It was just Joe Paterno's second year as the Penn State head coach.

It was like two different games., Penn State dominated the first half and at the break, led 17-0. Things were all FSU in the second half. Early on during the second half, FSU drove to the Penn State one yard line but failed to score. Later in the third quarter, Penn State faced with a fourth down and inches from its own fifteen yard line made, perhaps, the biggest mistake ever in Joe Paterno's career when it decided to go for it. An FSU defense stuffed an attempted quarterback sneak and the Seminoles got the ball back.

A FSU Hammond to Sellers pass shortly thereafter resulted in a touchdown. A short time later, FSU added another touchdown and the score was then locked at 17-14 where it stayed until the final moments of the game. Then FSU spoiled the game for PSU. FSU made its way to the Penn State eight yard line. On fourth down, with less than thirty seconds left on the clock, FSU's Grant Guthrie kicked a field goal and the game ended in a remarkable 17-17 tie. That was it for 1967 in JoPa's second season.

1968 Penn State Football Season Coach Joe Paterno – Championship??

The 1968 Penn State Nittany Lions football team was coached by Joe Paterno in his third season. The 1968 team was Paterno's first perfect season. He had gone from 5-5 to 8-2-1, to 11-0, and still could not get the pundits, the scribes or the coaches to give Penn State the championship it deserved. No matter what you think of the BCS, this is the scenario that it was created to avoid. This folks was a national championship season, no doubt.

Was it fair the Penn State was denied the National Championship with a perfect record and eleven games played? How about going 11–0? Regardless of the fairness factor, the voters ruled. The Nittany Lions finished behind 9–0 Ohio State and 9–0–1 USC in both polls. Not fair for sure. PSU should claim a piece of this championship as many other schools have done when fairness was not achieved. Just a thought. Every game was a win in 1968. Every game, including the big Orange Bowl game on January 11, 1969

On September 21, a # 10 ranked Navy team lost at Beaver Stadium to Penn State in a convincing match W (31-6). After the game, PSU was ranked # 4. Kansas State then played at Beaver Stadium on September 28, and were beaten handily W (25-9). West Virginia then played a #3 ranked PSU at Mountaineer Field and lost the game to a powerful PSU team W (31-20).

PSU then played UCLA in California on October 12 and beat the Bruins for the fourth win of the season W (21-6). Somehow after this victory, Penn State had slipped down one notch to # 4 in the polls. Who knows why? After a week bye, PSU played at Boston College's Alumni Stadium in Chestnut Hill, MA, and won a shutout W (29-0) against the Eagles.

Army, always tough, were not tough enough in a really tough game to beat Penn State. The Lions won this close match W (28-24) before 49,653, a virtual sellout of the original Beaver Stadium. After these two wins, PSU was still in 4th place.

Regardless of the polls, Penn State could not have won this game against Army without a little intervention. Surely many were praying as it came down to an onside kick.

All-America tight end Ted Kwalick swooped up the football coming out of a pile of players on an onside kick attempt in this game with 2:29 left. Kwalick was not an All-American by acclamation. He had earned it. In this game, the tight end took the ball in addition to all hopes for an Army victory across the goal line 53-yards after he had snagged the kick in the air. This was a very important touchdown for the 1968 season as it avoided an upset that would have ruined Penn State's first undefeated season under Paterno.

Remaining 1999 Games

Always tough national power Miami played PSU at Beaver Stadium on November 9 and lost W (22-7). The crowd was more than capacity at 50,132. On November 16 at Maryland, a then-ranked #3

PSU won big W (57–13). Still not able to budge the pundits or the coaches who had something else on their mind, PSU smothered a tough Pitt Panther team on November 23 at Pittsburgh W (65-9). Even big scores against college powerhouses could not move the Lions up in the rankings.

The Nittany Lions were still ranked at # 3, though undefeated and untied when a tough Syracuse team came to Beaver Stadium on December 7. It was a respectable game W (30-12) but clearly PSU dominated against the national power Syracuse squad. Played before 41,393 at Beaver Stadium. Penn State, a team accustomed to cold Pennsylvania winters beat a cold-weather team that had yet to gain the comforts of the Carrier Dome. December 7 was a cold day and if I may after the game with the rankings, it appeared that it would have to be an even colder day in Hell for Penn State to get a break, and if not a break, some fairness.

Yes, the PSU Syracuse encounter was a tough cold game. Somebody, someplace, however was warm enough to be pleading the case for some other teams to advance in the standings while PSU was neutralized. PSU did not move up a nickel in the polls all season long. Everybody knew the PSU schedule when shortly after the season began PSU was ranked # 3.

Moreover, though the PSU record was about as good as it could get in football, at 10-0, PSU's opponent for the Orange Bowl was not either of the # 1 or # 2 ranked teams in America and neither had as good a record as the Nittany Lions.

As an independent, perhaps the conferences dominated the post-season voting for opportunities. Playing # 6 Kansas, a fine team in 1967, would in no way nudge the PSU record up a notch so PSU could play for the championship. Even if the battle between the # 1 and # 2 at the time found both teams losing, the obvious bias of the press and the coaches, I regret to say would still have denied PSU its due.

The university does not complain but perhaps it should. Nothing is over until it is over. The deck was stacked against PSU by a set of biased coaches and biased pundits. Who knows? Maybe they simply did not like Pennsylvania or perhaps it was third year coach Joe

Paterno, who nobody knew because he was so new and thus did not deserve a championship. You tell me? Maybe somebody had an issue with Rip Engle or Bib Higgins or perhaps the Hollenback brothers that needed to be atoned. My only excuse is that it sure seems that some set of coaches and pundits with a relationship with a past Penn State coach or team believed they had experienced some animus that now had its chance to be righted. Again, who knows?

Quarterback Chuck Burkhart directed Penn State to its first two undefeated seasons under Joe Paterno in 1968 and '69. In the 1969 Orange Bowl against Kansas (above), Burkhart ran for a three-yard touchdown with eight seconds left and Bob Campbell's two-point run gave Penn State one of its most thrilling victories in program history, 15-14, to cap an 11-0 season and No. 2 finish in the Associated Press poll.

Nonetheless, Kansas and Penn State entered the Orange Bowl for this NBC televised game on January 1, 1969, both wanting to win this prestigious game and both hoping for the best. Both were great teams and nobody could deny that. Before 77,719 fans, Penn State played one of its best games ever against a very, very tough and respectable Kansas squad. PSU won the line battle and the scoring battle but just about won the game by one point W (15-14). Undefeated and untied—a championship for sure but not officially.

1969 Penn State Football Season Coach Joe Paterno Championship??

The 1969 Penn State Nittany Lions football team was coached by Joe Paterno in his fourth season. The 1968 team was Paterno's second perfect season in a row. He had gone from 5-5 to 8-2-1, to 11-0, and now again in 1969, 11-0, and yet the coaches and the pundits denied Penn State a National Championship for the second time in a row. As I have said before, no matter what you may think of the BCS, this is the scenario of which it was created.

Despite posting its second consecutive undefeated, untied season, the Nittany Lions did not have a fair shot at the national championship. Somehow President Richard Nixon was polled about his thinking on the matter. He said that he would consider the winner of the December 6 matchup between the Texas Longhorns and the Arkansas Razorbacks, then ranked at the top of the polls as the champion.

The coaches and the pundits mysteriously agreed with the President and they set up a scenario from which Penn State could again not compete in a championship game on New Year's Day. Sometimes even though a university does not whine, it should. PSU should have received a share of two national titles that it had earned.

Though there are no real excuses for this travesty against fair play, national champions were selected before the bowl games were played in January. Joe Paterno, who was a great speaker and a great teller of great stories—at the 1973 PSU Commencement ceremonies four years later, was quoted: "I've wondered how President Nixon could know so little about Watergate in 1973 and so much about college football in 1969." This was a national sham.

Pennsylvania Governor Raymond Shafer got into the act and quickly got the White House's attention with Penn State's 2 season undefeated streak. Shafer quickly declared that Pennsylvania State University was the # 1 team in the nation.

A White House assistant called Paterno to invite him and the team to the White House to receive a trophy for their accomplishment. Paterno has stated many times that he responded with, "You can tell the president to take that trophy and shove it." Penn State and the entire state of Pennsylvania declined an invitation to play the Texas/Arkansas winner in the Cotton Bowl.

When Nixon named Texas the national champion over Penn State

President Nixon's decision to name Texas the 1969 national champion over Penn State is explored in ESPN Film

As we review the 1969 season, it helps to remember that now, many years later, there will be no drama reading the season's games as each and every game was won by Penn State. Not all games were blow-outs but there were many, but Penn State won all the games –the shutouts, the blow-outs, and the close-calls, one after another. Every game below that you read about was a victory for Penn State though these wins were not enough for the coach's and pundits who perhaps wanted a different team or coach to win the national prize. It sure was not right. Then again, that's why today we have the BCS

The first win came on September 20 at Navy at the Navy-Marine Corps Memorial Stadium • Annapolis, MD. PSU was rated # 3 to start. The Nittany Lions won the game handily W (45–22) before 28,796. On September 27, Colorado came to play a now # 2 ranked PSU at Beaver Stadium and lost the game W (7–3) with 51,402 in attendance. On October 4, Kansas State hosted PSU at KSU Stadium for a close Lions win W (17–14). By Beating Kansas somehow PSU went down 3 notches in the polls to # 5. On October 11, #17 West Virginia tried to move up in the polls by beating now #5 ranked PSU at Beaver Stadium but the Nittany Lions shut out the Mountaineers W (20-0).

On October 18, Ben Schwartzwalder's tough Syracuse team hosted #5 ranked, unbeaten and untied Penn State and gave the Lions quite a tussle but PSU prevailed W (15-14) After Syracuse, ranked # 8, yet still unbeaten and still untied, PSU played Ohio on October 25, at Beaver Stadium and beat the Buckeyes by a pile W (42-3), bringing back the reward of a return to #5 in the polls. At Boston College on week 7, November 1, PSU defeated the Eagles W (38-16) at Beaver Stadium before 46,652.

On November 15, after a bye week, PSU smothered Maryland at home W 4(8-0). Now #4 ranked PSU played Pitt and beat the Panthers at Pitt Stadium W (27-7). On November 29, Carter Stadium was the home for a match-up of North Carolina State v # 3 ranked PSU, still unbeaten and untied with a 9-0 record going into game 10 of the season. Penn State convincingly beat the Wolfpack W (33-8).

It looked like Ohio State would automatically be the National Championship as they were ranked # 1 and were precluded from a Bowl game so no matter what when the Bowl decision had to be made, PSU only had a chance if Ohio State lost its last game. The decision had to be made before the last game, however.

Joe Paterno admitted that he liked the way the team was treated the previous year in Miami for the Orange Bowl, but he always thought you should play the best team you could.

That means that at the time the highest ranked team in the Bowl game which when the game was played would have been either Texas or Arkansas in the Cotton Bowl. Yet, the players decided to go to Miami. When Ohio lost, it made the Cotton Bowl the battle for the National Championship or so it seemed to the coaches and pundits. Penn State and the people of Pennsylvania and Governor Schaeffer felt otherwise.

Ranked #6 Missouri put up a fight but were defeated by the #2 ranked Penn State Nittany Lions in the Cotton Bowl. Texas beat Arkansas and were crowned National Champions. Penn State finished the balloting at # 2.

1970 Penn State Football Season Coach Joe Paterno

The 1970 Penn State Nittany Lions football team was coached by Joe Paterno in his fifth season, and continued to play its home games in Beaver Stadium in University Park, Pennsylvania. After two undefeated and untied seasons, 1970 was a rebuilding season but well played nonetheless. Paterno's Lions finished with a 7-3 record, ranked #19 in the coach's polls and #18 in the AP pundits poll.

Jack Ham—a standout at Linebacker U.

Ham, Jack Raphael (nickname Dobre Shunka)
Born: December 23, 1948, in Johnstown, Pennsylvania
Vocations: Athlete, Radio Personality, Sports Analyst

Kendle, fall 2007.

Short Bio: Jack Raphael Ham, Jr. was born in Johnstown, Pennsylvania, on December 23, 1948. He attended The Pennsylvania State University where he became one of the school's all-time great football players. He then went on to a wildly successful career in the National Football League with the Pittsburgh Steelers. After retiring, he entered broadcasting and headed a drug-testing company. He currently resides in Pittsburgh with his wife, Joanne.

Here is a bit more of the full "skinny" on Jack Ham. This biography was prepared by Wesley

Jack Ham, a man who would leave his mark on the world of American Football, was born in Johnstown, Pennsylvania, on December 23, 1948. The undersized and underrated linebacker graduated Bishop McCort High School in 1967 and found that he had no place to go. Ham, worried that his football career might be finished, then went to Massanutten Military Academy in Woodstock, Virginia, with hopes of toughening up and honing his skills in order to work his way onto a college football team.

Just when Ham had thought his only option was to enroll as a student at The Pennsylvania State University and attempt to walk on to the football team, his high school friend Steve Smear convinced recruiter George Welsh to offer Ham a newly opened scholarship. The rest is history. Jack Ham would go on to an astounding career in football, both with The Pennsylvania State University and the NFL's Pittsburgh Steelers. He is now considered to be one of American football's greatest linebackers to ever play the position.

1971 Penn State Football Season Coach Joe Paterno

The 1971 Penn State Nittany Lions football team was coached by Joe Paterno in his sixth season. If the man, who would soon be known and loved as JoePa knew anything at all, he knew how to win. With just one loss in an 11-1 season, I was a justified whiner in 1971 when for this stellar record, PSU was ranked at just #11 in the coach's poll and # 5 in the AP. A lot of coaches seemed to be unwilling to reward Penn State in the mid twentieth century for its valid accomplishments.

Joe Paterno's worst season so far was his first at 5-5. When any coach could follow this with 8-2-1; 11-0; 11-0; 7-3; and 11-1 records, that is one heck of a Division I coach. It is not coincidental that Joe Paterno is currently the winningest coach in the history of major league Division I football. Can you believe this fantastic start to a fantastic coaching career?

1972 Penn State Football Season Coach Joe Paterno Sugar Bowl

The 1972 Penn State Nittany Lions football team was coached by Joe Paterno in his seventh season. Penn State had another enviable regular season at 10-1 and with a #5 ranking in the national poll, they were invited to the Sugar Bowl in New Orleans against # 2 Oklahoma, and were defeated in a close match L (14-0), finishing the season at 10-2.

PSU Player Highlights: Franco Harris and Lydell Mitchell

What a blessing for any team to have Franco Harris and Lydell Mitchell playing in your backfield. One might ask if linemen would be necessary at all. Just kidding—honest! I can't complain because in my short high school football career I played guard and linebacker. Sure wish I had gone to Linebacker U at Penn State. Tteammates (FB) Franco Harris and (RB) Lydell Mitchell were outstanding.

Running backs and fullbacks did well at Penn State. We'll look at both running superstars from 1971. Let's look at the guy called on to get the 1st downs first and then the guy called on to win the games—Franco Harris then Lydell Mitchell

Franco Harris

Harris was a three-year starter and standout player for the Nittany Lions. Harris is a gentle yet very tough man. He still does not let anybody, including the press push his Alma Mater or his coach around. He hits back and stings and then continues to fight back

Nonetheless, he was one heck of a PSU football player even though I cannot find him on anybody's top ten PSU player list. He is on mine for sure.

When you dig down into Harris's great career at Penn State there was a player on the team who cast a big shadow. Fellow running back Lydell Mitchell became an All-American. Despite Mitchell's great stats the Steelers scouts still saw enough in Harris's play to draft him with their 13th overall selection of the 1972 NFL draft.

Harris gained more yards as a pro in his first season than in any of his Penn State Seasons, in which of course, he averaged between 5 and 6 yards per carry. He rushed for 1,055 yards and scored 10 touchdowns in his first year in the NFL and he was named Offensive Rookie of the Year and chosen for his first of nine consecutive Pro Bowls.

Harris is most famous for "The Immaculate Reception" in the AFC playoffs against the Oakland Raiders and was voted to the NFL 1970s All-Decade Team. Harris finished his Hall of Fame career with 100 touchdowns and 12,120 rushing yards.

Undoubtedly this reception is one of the greatest moments and the most talked about moments in football history. It is the nickname given to what is what most living pundits today would agree is the most famous play in the history of American football.

The game opponents were the Oakland Raiders vs the Pittsburgh Steelers with help from Franco Harris, and some say, help from the Lord himself. Even three Rivers Stadium could not prevent the miracle that was to occur on this Merry Christmas day December 23, 1972. Then, again if God is a Pittsburgh fan who had to worry?

Despite all of the spirits and the entire Franco Harris family and perhaps even a few Bradshaw's rooting for the right outcome, Pittsburgh was losing. So, with 30 seconds left in the game, Pittsburgh quarterback Terry Bradshaw, who still has lots of sputter during NFL game days, threw a "pass" attempt to John Fuqua. I cannot name one person today who knows who John Fuqua is but the ball did not reach him anyway.

It bounced off the hands of Raiders safety Jack Tatum; the world then went into slow-mo. as everybody in the stadium and watching from TV sets across the land, saw the ball falling toward the ground like a rocket. Like a gift from the most-high, out of nowhere, Steelers fullback Franco Harris, who had purchased a discount halo helmet attachment the night before the game at K-Mart, was there to scoop it up, right into his arms before ground-touch, and then as a schooled running back, the young Harris had enough sense and wherewithal to tuck it in and he ran for the game-winning touchdown. And, that was that. Everybody accepted the outcome. Well, not exactly.

No play that starts off so needy goes so far south without a miracle intervention from above. Even the agnostics did not know what had hit them. This play remains a source of unresolved controversy and speculation ever since, as many people have contended that the ball touched either Fuqua or the ground before Harris caught it, either of which would have resulted in an incomplete pass by the rules at the time.

Kevin Cook's *The Last Headbangers* cites the play as the beginning of a bitter rivalry between Pittsburgh and Oakland that fueled a historically brutal Raiders team during the NFL's most controversially physical era. Either way, Pittsburgh won and Harris got another TD...one of many in his outstanding career.

Another great back-- Lydell Mitchell

Though he played football and graduated in 1972, Lydell Mitchell was elected into the SBC Cotton Bowl Hall of Fame on December 20, 2004 with the major tribute being his 146-yard running total in the 1972 Cotton Bowl win over Texas.

Lydell Mitchell was an outstanding PSU football player. He was a

1971 All-American. As a dangerous running back, he led the Nittany Lions to a resounding 30-6 victory over Southwest Conference champion Texas in the Cotton Bowl on January 1, 1972. He pulled it in for 146 yards on 27 carries and scored the go-ahead touchdown, as Penn State rallied from a 6-3 halftime deficit to score 27 unanswered points in the second half. It was nothing less than the Lydell Mitchell Show with fullback Franco Harris picking up the slack as needed.

Lydell Mitchell was so good that the pundits did not fully notice Franco Harris but the Pittsburgh Steelers did. Mitchell led the nation in touchdowns (29) and points scored (174) in 1971. He also set three NCAA season records during his superlative 1971 campaign - most touchdowns (29), most rushing touchdowns (26) and points scored (174) - and finished fifth in the Heisman Trophy balloting. Franco Harris, one of the best football players in PSU history was kept in the shadows as the high-scoring Mitchell scored and scored and scored. On Dec. 7, 2004, Mitchell became the 19th Penn Stater to be inducted into the National Football Foundation's College Hall of Fame. Think about how great Lydell Mitchell was and think about how great Franco Harris was. Consider that Joe Paterno was their coach and he got the most out of them and they loved him for it.

Ted Kwalick

Ted Kwalick was inducted into the Polish American Hall of Fame on June 9, 2005. Having three children of Polish descent and living in a Polish / Irish family, I can say that I believe that Ted Kwalick enjoyed this honor as much as his College Hall of Fame induction.

Kwalick after the Maryland Game

In 1972, Kwalick scored nine touchdowns and averaged an amazing 18.8 yards per catch. After six seasons with the 49ers he played his last three years with the Oakland Raiders. In 1977, the Raiders beat the Vikings in Super Bowl XI giving Kwalick his Super Bowl ring. Kwalick was inducted into the College Football Hall of Fame in 1989.

As an aside, the all-time great lefty quarterback Kenny Stabler was steering the Raiders ship at that time. Ted Kwalick was the guy on the end of the defensive line getting the ball back for him to play another set off downs. Guys like "Snake" Stabler at QB made pro football at the time almost as interesting as college ball.

Sugar Bowl

The Sugar Bowl was played on December 31. PSU was ranked #5 with a 10-1 record when it met second ranked Oklahoma at Tulane Stadium in New Orleans before 80,123 and before million more on ABC TV. In one of its closest matches all season, Oklahoma defeated PSU L (14-0). This gave the Lions a nice 10-2 season, which for a number of reasons, could have been better.

Oklahoma had its second great year in a row under head coach Chuck Fairbanks. Offensive coordinator Barry Switzer had perfected the wishbone offense and Oklahoma could not be stopped. In 1971, the Sooners led the nation in both scoring (45 points average) and total yards (563 total yards' average).

Oklahoma set an NCAA record that year by averaging over 472.4 (5196 in 11 games) rushing yards in a season. The Sooners had another like year in 1972. They were phenomenal, and ran through every team they played.

There was a big discrepancy regarding the Sooners' record and the wins for which they got credit. It turns out that the NCAA never officially forced Oklahoma to forfeit games, but they were penalized on future scholarships. TV appearances, bowl appearances, etc. By rights, their team may not have been as good if their academic record keeping on their players was kept accurately.

The beef was that Oklahoma had used players (including Kerry Jackson, the team's first black quarterback) with falsified transcripts. It was such a big deal and such an embarrassment that at one point, Oklahoma University volunteered to forfeit all its games for the 1972 season.

Eventually, the Big Eight conference asked them to forfeit just three victories despite the fact that the NCAA still recognized them after time passed. Oklahoma in looking back, now recognizes all of its wins and it claims the 1972 conference title. Penn State was involved in the controversy as a team that had played an Oklahoma that had benefitted from using ineligible players.

At the time, as a result of using ineligible players, the Oklahoma Sooners were apparently ordered (though it was softened to a suggestion over time) to forfeit seven wins from their 1972 season, including their on-field win over the Nittany Lions in the Sugar Bowl. Joe Paterno's Nittany Lions were shut-out L (14-0) as noted but they had played a tough game against the Sooners.

Despite the prevailing thought on the legitimacy of the Sooners' season, Joe Paterno and the Penn State Administration refused to accept the forfeit, and the bowl game is officially recorded as a loss. There is some irony compared with how Coach Paterno was treated when it was his turn in the penalty box in 2011. Paterno, just about forty years earlier opted not to mess with Oklahoma's wins and losses.

Who knows if the QB and some other players made a difference? PSU had a shot at being 12-1 instead of 11-2. Who knows what that would have meant? Penn State was not interested in being handed any gifts that it had not earned on the field. As it turned out, officially PSU is listed as # 8 in the coach's poll and #10 in the AP poll.

1973 Penn State Football Season Coach Joe Paterno Championship ??

The 1973 Penn State Nittany Lions football team was coached by Joe Paterno in his eighth season. Penn State had another **undefeated and untied** season just four years after having two undefeated and untied seasons in a row. Despite having a perfect 12-0 season, PSU for the third time in six years was denied a proper ranking by the Coaches and by the AP. They slotted Penn State at # 5 after its third perfect season in six years. No wonder many felt that the system was rigged.

When like me, one walks slowly through the Paterno record—in my case because I am forming words and scribing it; in your case, as you are reading my words, you get the full sense of what an awesome achievement it was for the University, the players involved, and this awesome coach. Looking at the results season by season, nobody was as good as Joe Paterno in his eight seasons. You'd have to look outside of Penn State in 1973 to find a Rockne or a Leahy to match the outstanding record of Joe Paterno.

Penn State's third undefeated season under Joe Paterno was led by John Cappelletti who would become the first Penn State player to win the Heisman Trophy.

In an early season start on September 15, at Stanford #7 PSU defeated the Cardinal W (20-6). At Navy on September 22, PSU shut out the Middies W (39-0. At # 6 on September 29, the Nittany Lions played its home opener and scored a win against Iowa W (27-8). At Falcon Stadium on October 6, PSU beat the Falcons W (19-9).

Ironically after the win, PSU lost a point in the standings. The #7 Lions battered a game Army squad on October 13 at Beaver Stadium on October 20 W (54-3) Off to Archbold Stadium in Syracuse, #5 PSU beat the Orangemen W (49-6) After winning game after game, the 6-0 Nittany Lions would never get above # 5 in the polls for the rest of the season. It was as if other teams had a lock on the top 4 slots.

On October 27, West Virginia was roughed up by a tough Lions Team W 62-14 before an over-crowd of 59,138, an expansion built in in 1972 had brought capacity to 57,538. On November 3 #6 PSU defeated Maryland at Byrd Stadium W (42-22).

This was followed by a close win on November 10 at home against NC State W (35-9).

In this best of Beaver Stadium game, John Cappelletti, #22, solidified his credentials for the Heisman Trophy with his best running day ever in this wild shootout in freezing cold and snow. Cappelletti set a school record of 41 carries that is still unbroken in rushing for 231 yards and three touchdowns.

Ohio University was next at Beaver Stadium on November 17 W (49-10) At 10-0, ranked # 6, PSU played Pittsburgh at home and defeated the Panthers W (35-13).

The powers-that-be saw something that few at Penn State saw. These mysterious powers felt it appropriate to match the powerful 11-0, #5 ranked Nittany Lions against a twice beaten 9-2, #13 LSU in the Orange Bowl on January 1. PSU defeated LSU W (16-9). PSU ended its perfect season 12-0 and LSU finished with three defeats 9-3. It may not have been the Nittany Lions finest game but one thing is for sure. Joe Paterno knew how to win football game.

Orange Bowl Game Highlights

The Undefeated Penn State Nittany Lions moved its record to 12-0 on the season as it took advantage of consistently poor LSU field position to win 16-9.

LSU had a good game as it out-gained the Nittany Lions 274 yards to 185 and held Heisman Trophy winner John Cappelletti to 50 yards. Cappelletti nonetheless was the difference maker as he scored the Nittany Lions' final touchdown on a one-yard plunge in the second quarter. The game's big play was a spectacular 72-yard touchdown catch by Chuck Herd off a pass from Tom Shuman early in the second quarter.

LSU got a lot of yardage but not of lot scores. The Tigers scored first on a three-yard run by Steve Rogers, and Penn State retaliated with a 44-yard field goal by Chris Bahr to make it 7-3 at the end of the first quarter. Herd's catch and Cappelletti's plunge put PSU ahead 16-7 at the half. That was the game.

Although Penn State finished undefeated, the polls still had the Nittany Lions ranked at #5.

1974 Penn State Football Season Coach Joe Paterno Cotton Bowl

The 1974 Penn State Nittany Lions football team was coached by Joe Paterno and played its home games in Beaver Stadium in University Park, Pennsylvania. At # 7 in both polls and with a 10-2 record, and a fine Cotton Bowl win, Penn State had a remarkably great year after so many previous great years. It's like the flow of great athletes would never stop.

The Cotton Bowl

With a 9-2 record, ranked # 7 ranked PSU won a berth to the Cotton Bowl and on New Year's Day, beat #12 Baylor in Dallas Texas before 67,500 onlookers as well as the entire CBS TV audience W (41–20).

Five times in their 10-victory season, the Nittany Lions came from behind to win. This particular New Year's Day in 1975 would become their sixth. For two and a half quarters, Baylor's Bears played like old hands before the Eastern powerhouse. The two teams traded first quarter turnovers before Baylor began its march to a 7-0 lead.

Moving the football really wasn't a problem for the Lions in the first half, but punching it across the goal line was. It wasn't until the clock ticked down to 1:13 in the half that Penn State finally cracked the scoreboard with a 25-yard Matt Bahr field goal. When play resumed in the third quarter, it was quarterback Tom Shuman's turn to shine, engineering an 80-yard Penn State drive that put them in the lead for the first time at 10-7.

Shuman threw strikes of 42 and 20 yards to his tight end Dan Natale to fuel the march, while Tom Donchez ended it with a one-yard plunge up the middle for a 10-7 lead. The Bears came roaring back in the waning minutes of the quarter to regain the lead when Jeffrey hit Ricky Thompson for 35 yards, making it a 14-10 ballgame. The seesaw battle continued.

With its next possession, Penn State took the lead for good. Starting from their 48, Donchez gained three on first down, and Shuman decided it was time to go deep. Freshman Jimmy Cefalo worked his way behind Baylor defensive back Scooter Reed and Shuman's pass was on the money. Cafalo made the grab at the nine and then cruised in for the score, 17-14.

It was more of the same in the fourth quarter. Penn State turned each possession into points: Cefalo scored from the three; Bahr hit another field goal; Shuman kept at left guard for two and the touchdown which made it 34-14; and linebacker Joe Jackson scooped up Baylor's outside kick on the last play of the game and ran 50 yards for the final score. Penn State's 41 points was a Classic record.

1975 Penn State Football Season Coach Joe Paterno Sugar Bowl

The 1975 Penn State Nittany Lions football team was coached by Joe Paterno in his tenth year. With a 9-2 regular season record and a berth in the Sugar Bowl at the New Orleans, Louisiana Superdome on December 31, 1975, PSU, with Joe Paterno, an unbelievably successful coach at the helm, had a great season. No Championship this year bu a lot of fine play.

Sugar Bowl

Alabama beat Penn State 13-6 in the New Years Eve Sugar Bowl in the Superdome. For this game, Bear Bryant had recommended Paterno's Nittany Lions as a worthy opponent for this game. Bryant forecasted a win: "I think we'll win," Bryant said, then hastily added, "if I don't overcoach 'em."

Alabama QB Richard Todd had suffered a Christmas-Day cut on his finger. He came out with the finger bandaged, and PSU literally dared him to throw. Overloading the line and hoping to force 'Bama into mistakes, Penn State paid an early price. Joe Dale Harris, a starter just because of curfew violations, ran a simple turn-in pattern that Todd got off just before being engulfed by the defense. There weren't enough Lions in the secondary to take all the receivers, and Harris was free, turning the short yardage pass into a 54-yard gain. That play eventually was converted into a 25-yard field goal by Danny Ridgeway and a 3-0 Alabama lead that held up to the half.

Chris Bahr tied things with a 42-yard field goal in the third quarter, but Todd brought the Tide roaring back, though admittedly he was never really sure of what he was doing against the ever-changing Penn State defense. Todd then lost four yards recovering a fumble, but Mike Stock swept into the end zone behind a ferocious block by Newsome.

Bahr cut the margin to 10-6 with a 37-yard field goal in the fourth quarter, but Ridgeway answered with a 28-yarder. With 3:19 left, Penn State got one last chance. The Nittany Lions inched out to their 39, where, on fourth-and-one, they went for it. Alabama held with 1:15 to go, and Bryant's bowl skein was broken. Penn State had lost the Sugar Bowl

1976 Penn State Football Season Coach Joe Paterno Gator Bowl Loss

The 1976 Penn State Nittany Lions football team was coached by Joe Paterno in his eleventh year and played its home games in a just expanded Beaver Stadium in University Park, Pennsylvania. In 1969, PSU found another 2000 seats for Beaver Stadium. In 1974, over 9000 seats, extended the capacity to 57,536. In 1976: South end zone bleachers expanded, adding 2,667, extending capacity to 60,203. Coming up in 1978, another big expansion of 16000 seats was coming and the growing still would not be done.

For any other program in any other year, Penn State's 7-5 record in 1976 would have been chalked up as well above .500 and very acceptable. Not for the Lions who always exceeded that mark under JoePa

1977 Penn State Football Season Coach Joe Paterno Fiesta Bowl Win

The 1977 Penn State Nittany Lions football team was coached by Joe Paterno in his twelfth season. PSU recovered from a tough 7-5 season and experienced one loss to Kentucky at home on October 1, the fourth game of the season by just four points L (20-24).

Four points doth make a season as the Kentucky game is all that separated Paterno's tough Penn State squad from another perfect, undefeated and untied, season. The one loss made all the difference in the world as the Nittany Lions finished #4 in the Coach's poll and #5 in the AP poll. It was another great year for Penn State on the field.

Penn State coach Joe Paterno and his quarterback Chuck Fusina discussed things late in the fourth quarter in Pittsburgh, Saturday, Nov. 26, 1977.

Fiesta Bowl

Penn State was always known for its shove-it-down-your-throat type football. Arizona State's style was a potent aerial assault. In the 1977 Fiesta Bowl, the Nittany Lions flexed their muscles in the second half to pull away from Arizona State, 42-30, in front of a record crowd of 57,727.

Both teams had their chances. But Penn State took advantage of every opportunity and then some to post the very exciting victory. The Nittany Lions turned a blocked punt and a fumble recovery into a pair of first quarter touchdowns to post a lead they would never relinquish.

Arizona State never gave up in the contest, pulling within three points just before halftime and trailing by only six points midway through the fourth quarter.

But the running of Penn State backs Steve Geise and Bob Torrey took its toll. Geise finished with 111 yards and a touchdown on 26 carries, while Torrey ran for 107 yards and a score on just nine carries. Matt Suhey added 76 yards and two touchdowns, as the Nittany Lions racked up 268 yards on the ground.

Quarterback Dennis Sproul had a solid game for ASU, completing 23 of 47 passes for 336 yards and three touchdowns. He was named the offensive player of the game and earned the first ever Art Bodine Sportsmanship Award, which was voted on by the officials.

1978 Penn State Football Season Coach Joe Paterno "Almost" Championship

The 1978 Penn State Nittany Lions football team was coached by Joe Paterno in his thirteenth year. This Chuck Fusina led-team was phenomenal. In 1977, four points to Kentucky in the fourth game separated PSU from a perfect season. This year, PSU did not lose a game until the Sugar Bowl when it was a seven-point difference against a Bear Bryant coached Alabama team that kept PSU from the National Championships.

PSU was 11-0 and ranked # 2 going into the game. Alabama was 11-0 and ranked #1. Alabama won the game and the National Championship. PSU finished 11-1 and were ranked # 4 in both polls. Joe Paterno was a phenomenon. SO was Bear Bryant. My buddy George Mohanco, a former Pennsylvanian has a saying, whether he invented it, I do not know but it applies to 1978. "Sometimes you eat the bear and sometimes the bear eats you." This time Bear Bryant had the better dinner.

Penn State started the season at # 3 with a game on September 3 at Veterans Stadium at Temple. Temple played extremely tough but the Lions got the W (10-7). This was a strange game. It was dominated by a typically unsung hero, punter Casey Murphy. Former Navy coach and relatively new Temple coach Wayne Hardin had Murphy punt "unexpectedly," on nearly every third down. Murphy averaged more than 48 yards on 11 punts. He backed up the surprised Penn State team inside its 6-yard line three times. PSU was fighting up-hill all day because of the Owls' punter

The Nittany Lions put together what it took to win W (10-7), but it was not easy. It was a late field goal. Joe Paterno honored Coach Hardin's cunning after the game: "That's the best coaching job anybody's done against us ever."

Rutgers was next at the newly enlarged (by 16,000 seats) Beaver Stadium on September 9 v #3 PSU. The Nittany Lions won W (26-10) in front of a newly enabled attendance of 77,154. Woody Hayes' # 6 ranked Ohio State Buckeyes expecting a win were turned back by # 5 ranked PSU at Ohio Stadium on September 16 W (19-0). SMU was defeated on September 23 at Beaver Stadium W (26-21).

TCU was blown away W (58-0) by #5 PSU on September 30. Kentucky, the team that spoiled the 1977 season with a four-point win were shown how it's done by # 4 PSU in an October 7 shutout in Lexington, KY W (30-0). After a bye week, Syracuse came into Beaver Stadium on October 21, and #2 PSU beat the Orangemen W (45-15). On October 28, the West Virginia Mountaineers were defeated by #2 PSU in a blowout at Morgantown, WV, W (49-21).

On November 4, 1978 in a home match at Beaver Stadium before 78,019, #2 ranked Penn State beat #5 ranked Maryland W (27-3). This was a nationally televised "Battle of the Unbeatens." It was the Nittany Lions' biggest--and most hyped--home game since the stadium was built in 1960. With 16,000 seats added since 1977, a record crowd of 78,019 watched No. 2 Lions overwhelm No. 5 Maryland, finally becoming a media darling in the race for the national championship.

Let's take a closer look at this game as it is one of the most memorable in PSU history. Maryland had a great team in 1978 and so did Penn State. Before they came to Beaver Stadium, the first Saturday in November, the Terrapins were rolling over their opposition.

Maryland Game

They were ranked # 5 with eight straight wins behind them. They had already pummeled NC State 31-7. NC State would finish ranked # 18. Maryland had the ACC title in the bag if they beat Penn State.

PSU for its part was doing so well at #2. Maryland might be looking at a national title with a win. PSU however was on a 16-game winning streak and as expected, the welcome for Maryland would not be warm, and the Lions were prepared to play tough.

Maryland got the ball first, and then they got a feel for Penn State's defense on a 3rd and 8. Bruce Clark and Matt Millen pounded Terrapin QB Tim O'Hare for a 1-yard loss and a punt. The Nittany Lions began to drive down a short field immediately with nice runs by backs Booker Moore and Matt Suhey. This ended with a Matt Bahr 33-yard field goal.

Booker Moore then fumbled but it did not hurt Penn State as the "D" got the ball right back. From there, Mike Guman caught a 14-yarder and a nice 34-yard run set up a Chuck Fusina 1-yard TD drive as the second quarter began. Maryland seemed to get some adrenalin going and quickly converted a 39-yard field goal.

With PSU now ahead by 7, they held the Terrapins on a tough 3-and-out, and then after the punt when it was PSU's turn, Bob Bassett's snagged a 22-yard one-handed grab which put PSU again in field goal position. Matt Bahr was an automatic and he claimed the three points for PSU. Although the powerful defense held Maryland to just 12 rushing yards, the Nittany Lions still led by just 13-3 at the half.

In the 3rd quarter Pete Harris got an interception and the Terrapins benched their QB and put in reserve Mike Tice. It seemed like a good move as Maryland took the ball deep into PSU territory, but the drive was thwarted by Karl McCoy's interception. Fusina finished off this drive by pin-pointing a 63-yard pass to Tom Donovan making the score Penn State 20, Maryland 3.

McCoy grabbed another interception late in the third, and before long Booker Moore gobbled up 34-yards on a scamper to the Maryland 16. Four plays later, Moore scored on a 4-yard run for the touchdown.

As the game was closing, Maryland's kept in their starters and came to a fourth and goal from the 3 but were denied the score by Penn State's backup unit. The underclassmen got a standing ovation from the Nittany Lions fans.

Penn State's defense had been dominant all season long and this day would be no different as they brought forth their best performance in the 27-3 victory over #5 Maryland in Beaver Stadium. It was the Lions 17th straight victory.

For his role in the game, QB Chuck Fusina made the cover of Sports Illustrated. As noted in this 1978 season record, PSU just got by North Carolina State and #15 Pittsburgh to become # 1 in the polls. Even after undefeated seasons, this was the first #1 ranking in Joe Paterno's already legendary career. As an independent, PSU could go just about anywhere for their bowl, so they picked the SEC for a match-up with #2 Alabama in the Sugar Bowl – discussed at the end of 1978 highlights below.

A tough North Carolina team played #2 ranked PSU at Beaver Stadium on November 11 and were beaten by the Lions in a close call W (19-10).

This 1978 game was a typical nail biter. No. 2 Penn State was holding on to a 12-10 lead with 4:40 left and with the crowd of 59,424 growing restless, Penn State's Matt Suhey (shown on the left) returned a punt 43 yards for a touchdown to clinch the victory.

As soon as Suhey scored, it was announced that #1 Oklahoma had lost three days later, and so Penn State was ranked #1 for the first time ever.

Operating with a 10-0 record, ranked #1 in the nation, for the first time ever, playing nemesis cross-state rival Pittsburgh, anything could have happened on November 24.

PSU was steady and steadfast in its resolve to win and the Nittany Lions shut-out Pitt W (17-0) at Beaver Stadium and had just enough offense to keep Pittsburgh from thinking it had a chance. For its 11-0 season PSU was ranked #1 but there was another team with an 11-0 record, looking up at PSU from the # 2 slot.

The Sugar Bowl 1978

Alabama, coached by the inimitable great, Bear Bryant, a man with the great coaching stature of Joe Paterno, with a great team, was ranked #2. The Sugar Bowl eventually got the #1 and # 2 teams to play each other even though Coach Paterno would have preferred the Orange Bowl, the last game played on New Year's Day. That did not happen. Destiny was in the hands of both teams.

With its 11-1 1977 season behind them coming in with just four points separating PSU from a National Championship bid, PSU had high expectations for the 1978 season. Before game time. Nobody could say that the 1978 Penn State squad had disappointed anybody. PSU had a great season after barely escaping Temple in game 1.

While some games were relatively close, the Nittany Lions generally won each game with ease. Its defense was #1 in the nation. This was a Paterno hallmark at Linebacker U. It held teams to ten points or less. #1 ranked PSU had made it to the gates of the national championship. The great 1978 Penn State football team was ready for a win.

Alabama also had great expectations coming into the 1978 season. In 1977, they too were 11-1 11–1, losing only to Nebraska. They had devastated Ohio State in the 1978 Sugar Bowl much to Woody Hayes' chagrin. They were third in the country coming into their bowl game. The two top teams lost and Alabama naturally believed that it rightfully had earned the honor of being national champions. Notre Dame had rolled over #1 Texas in the 1978 Cotton Bowl

Classic, and the Irish jumped from 5th to 1st to become national champions. The Crimson Tide felt robbed and it was their big motivation for 1978. There they were again with just PSU to get by. Alabama was also ready for a win.

And, so, this year's edition of the New Year's Day Sugar Bowl capped off the 1978 season and was the 45th edition of the Sugar Bowl, it was played in New Orleans, Louisiana on January 1, 1979 at the Louisiana Superdome. A close score of L (7-14) gave Alabama head coach Bear Bryant his fifth National Championship. After such a fine season, Joe Paterno was still looking for his first.

1979 Penn State Football Season Coach Joe Paterno

The 1979 Penn State Nittany Lions football team was coached by Joe Paterno. No team can have a championship every year. After back to back 11-1 seasons, PSU kept working hard. The University football program did not take the night off. Joe Paterno's squad compiled a 7-4 regular season record and won the Liberty Bowl, making the record 8-4. PSU was top-twenty ranked in both polls—#18 in the Coach's poll and #20 in the AP.

Liberty Bowl

On December 22, the unranked Nittany Lions beat # 15 ranked Tulane in the Liberty Bowl W (9-6). The game was played in Memorial Stadium in Memphis Tennessee before a crowd of 50,021 and a nationwide TV audience on ABC. After the Liberty Bowl victory, PSU moved back into the top twenty—#18 in the Coach's poll and #20 in the AP.

1980 Penn State Football Season Coach Joe Paterno

The 1980 Penn State Nittany Lions football team was coached by Joe Paterno in his fifteenth season with Penn State. The team had a great season, winning two more games than in 1979, and finishing with a 10-2 record, ranked #8 in both polls. I am in awe about how consistent a winner, coach Paterno was with his PSU teams. Bravo! No chmpionship but a great Bravo!

Matt Millen

Former player Matt Millen

Millen was a great Nittany Lion He was a sure fit in the NFL. In Millen's 12-year NFL playing career, he played on four teams that won the Super Bowl. Millen won a Super Bowl ring with each of the three teams for which he played; moreover, he won a Super Bowl ring in each of the four cities in which he played (the Raiders won championships in both Oakland and Los Angeles during his tenure).

Millen was president and CEO of the NFL Detroit Lions until 2008.

Chapter 17 Joe Paterno Era 1981 to 1995

Coach # 14

1981	Joe Paterno	10-2	
1982	Joe Paterno	11-1	National Champions
1983	Joe Paterno	8-4-1	
1984	Joe Paterno	6-5	
1985	Joe Paterno	11-1	
1986	Joe Paterno	12-0	National Champions
1987	Joe Paterno	8-4	
1988	Joe Paterno	5-6	
1989	Joe Paterno	8-3-1	
1990	Joe Paterno	9-3	
1991	Joe Paterno	11-2	
1992	Joe Paterno	7-5	
1993	Joe Paterno	10-2	(6-2 Big 10)
1994	Joe Paterno	12-0	(8-0 Big 10)
1995	Joe Paterno	9-3	(5-3 Big 10)

Coached 45 great seasons 1966 to 2010 and part of 2011.

1981 Penn State Football Season Coach Joe Paterno Fiesta Bowl win

The 1981 Penn State Nittany Lions football team was coached by Joe Paterno in his sixteenth season. Coach Joe Paterno did it again—a 9-

2 excellent regular season and a victory over USC in the Fiesta Bowl giving a 10-2 combined record and a #3 position in both polls.

On November 28, Penn State said enough is enough and shellacked #1 ranked Pittsburgh at Pitt Stadium W (48-14) in Dan Marino's last year. Incidentally, with Pitt's 11-1 record, PSU had put the only blemish on its season. The Pitt Team came back from the PSU loss, played and beat the # 2 team in the country Georgia 24-20 in the Sugar Bowl.

The Nittany Lions delivered one of their most satisfying wins when quarterback Tod Blackledge (above) and the defense sparked a turnaround from a 14-0 deficit to a 48-14 win at No. 1 Pitt on November 28, 1981. Penn State beat Southern California in th 1982 Fiesta Bowl to finish 10-2 and ranked No. 3, setting the table for the Nittany Lion. 1982 National Championship

On this day in 1981 Penn State pulled off one of its finest come from behind victories, snapping back from a 14-0 second-quarter deficit to rout No. 1 Pitt, 48-14, and end the national title chances of the Sugar Bowl-bound Panthers before a national television audience and 60,260 at Pitt Stadium. The victory was sparked by interceptions of Dan Marino passes by Roger Jackson and Mark Robinson and the passing combination of Todd Blackledge to Kenny Jackson.

Todd Blackledge

When I first saw Todd Blackledge play at the Carrier Dome v Syracuse years ago, I was amazed at the passing after having seen so many games in which Penn State would run the ball almost all the time even if the situation clearly called for a pass. Before Blackledge, it seemed Paterno was always squeamish about passing.

Penn State Football, Todd Blackledge

On this day v Pittsburgh facing the consummate passer of all time, Dan Marino, JoePa had to let Blackledge throw—but would he? He sure did. Not only did Coach OK a vaunted passing attack, it was as if PSU had been a passing team forever. Blackledge could not do anything wrong. He played one heck of a game

He was so good that Todd Blackledge upstaged the best passer in football Dan Marino at quarterback. Penn State got its biggest upset since Joe Paterno became the head coach in 1966, a huge 48-14 victory over top-ranked Pittsburgh that ended the Panthers' 17-game winning streak, and ended their day in the championship sun.

Marino was a junior at the time, and as the QB, so far in the game he had put Pitt out ahead so quickly that it looked like the crying towels would be needed. Marino had already thrown for two touchdowns to put the Panthers ahead by 14-0 in the first 10 minutes.

Blackledge, Penn State's sophomore quarterback got some breaks and took advantage of them. There were a series of Panther mistakes that in a flash turned the game around. Before the Panthers knew it, the game was tied and then they were losing.

Blackledge threw two touchdown passes to Kenny Jackson, ran for one touchdown and wound up with 12 completions in 23 attempts for 262 yards before a crowd of 60,260 in Pitt Stadium.

Blackledge was elated. "This was the best game of my life," he said. Marino was not his usual pinpoint self with 22 completions in 45 attempts for 267 yards. His big problem was that he got only 80 yards in the second half. He was intercepted four times and his team lost three fumbles. The seven turnovers killed the Panthers.

"We can't cry," said Marino, who had taken Pitt to be the #1 team in the nation with 34 touchdown passes before this day in this season. "They did a good job and beat us outright today. We just made too many mistakes, and you can't win with so many fumbles, penalties and interceptions."

Going back into the archives, the Nittany Lions had a tough time finding another such significant victory. They had to go back to 1964 when PSU shocked OSU, 27-0, and toppled the Buckeyes from the No. 1 rank in midseason.

Clemson had been ranked No. 2 before this day and became the only undefeated and untied major team in the nation. If Clemson moved up to No. 1 the following week in the two wire service polls, the Tigers would become the seventh team to hold the top spot this season. Pitt was the sixth team and Penn State was one of the others, along with Michigan, Notre Dame, Southern California and Texas. All were beaten and had dropped from the top spot.

Penn State, which finished the regular season at (9-2), was ranked 11th by The Associated Press and ninth by United Press International going into the game. The Nittany Lions, scheduled for the Fiesta

Bowl would be preparing to play Southern California on Jan. 1, the same day Pitt (10-1) would be play Georgia (9-1) in the Sugar Bowl.

The outcome of this upset was unclear. It made it possible for Georgia, last year's final No. 1 team, to gain the No. 1 ranking again, barring an upset the next Saturday against Georgia Tech. The Bulldogs, ranked No. 3 before all the games on this day, were expected to move up to No. 2 behind Clemson, which would be playing Nebraska in the Orange Bowl Jan. 1. If Nebraska won and Pitt lost in bowl action, Georgia could be No. 1.

Pitt was a one-touchdown favorite over PSU going into today's game. Coming out, the Panthers' had suffered their first loss since, and a big one, since they were beaten by Florida State in the fifth game of the 1980 season. The triumph was Paterno's 150th as Penn State head coach against 33 losses and one tie. His two losses this particular season came against Miami and Alabama. Not an Upset, Says Paterno.

Paterno, an assistant coach at Penn State when the Lions beat Ohio State 17 years prior, said: "I didn't think this was an upset. Who says so?"

One of his former players, Irv Pankey, an offensive tackle on Penn State's 1978 team, added, "This without a doubt is the best victory ever." Pankey, then a member of the Los Angeles Rams, was at the game because the Rams were to meet the Steelers at Three Rivers Stadium Sunday.

Penn State stopped Pitt with an interception and a fumble recovery the next two times the Panthers had the ball and the Lions took over on their 20 late in the second period. Blackledge completed three successive passes to get to the 7. The third of these was a 53-yard toss to Jackson.

Blackledge went in from there on a quarterback draw that caught Pitt with a huge defensive hole right in the middle.

Warner pressed into duty

Curt Warner, Penn State's best tailback, did not start the game because of recent leg injuries. But when Jon Williams also got hurt early in the game, Warner came in and ran for 104 yards to finish his junior season with 1,044 yards rushing. He had missed two full games and most of two others this season.

Coach Sherrill said, "They outplayed us simply and we made too many mistakes. Next one is against Georgia."

When it was all over, PSU was # 3 in both post season polls whereas Pitt was # 2 in the Coach's poll and #4 in the AP poll. Texas, which had a loss and a tie played Clemson and lost but yet, was given the #4 slot in the Coach's Poll and were ranked above Pitt at # 2 in the AP poll. The Clemson Tigers, who were unbeaten and untied, claimed the national championship with #1 ranking in both polls after their victory over Nebraska in the Orange Bowl. No wonder we have the BCS today.

In the 1983 NFL Draft, Kansas City selected Blackledge seventh overall. He played for the Chiefs for five seasons before joining the Pittsburgh Steelers in 1988. He retired in 1989.

1982 Penn State Football Season Coach Joe Paterno

The 1982 Penn State Nittany Lions football team was coached by Joe Paterno in his seventeenth season. After a disappointing loss at Birmingham to #4 Alabama in game 5 L (21-42), a resilient and very tough Penn State squad came back and brought home all the marbles. The Nittany Lions won every game for the rest of the regular season, and defeated the #1 Georgia Bulldogs 27–23 in the Sugar Bowl. Added to their 11-1 record Penn State's fine play gave Joe Paterno his first consensus national championship.

Watching the season records grow over the years, I still cannot get over how many games Paterno won and we are only in his seventeenth season. In 1982, JoePa was just in his mid-50. He surely knew how to get the most out of his players. That is the job of a great coach. Another great coach, Frank Leahy, at Notre Dame, a bit before Paterno's time, had a saying that I think was the same type of saying JoePa would use to get the most out of his lads. Leahy said: "Lads, you're not to miss practice unless your parents died or you died." That about says it all!

On September 11, # 7 ranked PSU defeated Maryland at Beaver Stadium in a very close game W (39-31). On September 18Rutgers played a # 8 ranked Penn State and lost by a mile W (49-14).

2 Nebraska, coached by the Great Tom Osborne, with his own share of national championships, always a tough team played #8 PSU at Beaver Stadium on September 25. Osborne's team got its only loss (W (27-24) of the season in a very close game.

There are those that have this game characterized as the greatest game ever at Beaver Stadium. See write-up under picture on next page.

On October 9, came the loss at Alabama L (21-42). Alabama lost four of its next seven games which took them way out of the hunt for the championship.

Always ready to create havoc with a great PSU season, Syracuse played the #8 Nittany Lions at Beaver Stadium and lost W (28-7). West Virginia played #9 PSU in Mountaineer Stadium and gave up a loss W (24-0). Alumni Stadium in Chestnut Hill (Boston) was the scene for #8 PSU to shellack the unranked Eagles W (52-17). On November 7, #7 PSU then shut out and literally pounded NC State at Beaver Stadium W (54-0). #13 Notre Dame hosted # 5 PSU on November 13, as Penn State needed every win to have a shot at a championship. In a close match, #5 PSU (8-1) outplayed Notre Dame and got the W (24-14)

PSU v ND 1982

Yogi Berra may not have been a football player but his saying that it ain't over 'til it's over rand true in the 1982 matchup between Notre Dame and Penn State. In 1982, the Irish were coming off a 31-16 upset over then-No. 1 Pittsburgh when the No. 5 Lions came to South Bend.

September 25, 1982—Penn State 27, Nebraska 24: This was the greatest game ever at Beaver Stadium as quarterback Todd Blackledge led a come-from-behind 65-yard drive in 10 plays with 1:14 left and no timeouts to beat No. 3 Nebraska. His controversial 15-yard sideline pass to Mike McCloskey at the two-yard-line with nine seconds remaining and subsequent touchdown pass to Kirk Bowman had the record crowd of 85,304 celebrating inside and outside the lighted stadium for hours. ¶

Historical Nick Gancitano (Penn State) Field Goal against Notre Dame 1982

Notre Dame scored first, but a one-yard run by quarterback Todd Blackledge and two field goals by Nick Gancitano put the Lions up 13-7. Freshman sensation Pinkett, who would go on to have his best games of his career against the Lions, took a kickoff 93 yards for a touchdown and a 14-13 ND lead.

Blackledge, however, responded with a 48-yard-scoring strike to Curt Warner and Penn State went on to a 24-14 victory en route to its first national championship.

At 10-1, on November 26 # 2 Penn State played a tough #5 Pittsburgh at Beaver Stadium. The Nittany Lions controlled the game and won W (19-10). Penn State was the #2 team in the nation and they got a chance in the Sugar Bowl to play the #1 ranked team.

This year's Sugar Bowl was the type of game from which they make movies. The game would determine the 1982 national champions unless both teams played like pikers, which was highly unlikely for the recognized two best teams in the nation.

Georgia had a tough schedule and the Bulldogs had not lost a game. At 11-0, they thought they were pretty good. Penn State at 10-1, with a non-sequitur loss to Alabama felt pretty good about themselves. The game itself, for the first time in many trips to the great field for Penn State and Joe Paterno, would determine the national champion. Win, you're in; Lose, you're out and probably not even #2!

The game was played in the Louisiana Superdome in New Orleans, LA. It was called the Sugar Bowl but neither team had decided to sweeten anything for their opponent. Penn State at # 2, Georgia at #1—it was a game scheduled by the gods. And so, it happened on January 1, 1983 that the Pennsylvania State Nittany Lions defeated the great Georgia Bulldogs in a phenomenally tough football game W (19-10). 85,522 attendees plus a national ABC TV football audience enjoyed the game. Only half, my half, thankfully, enjoyed the score.

1983 Penn State Football Season Coach Joe Paterno

The 1983 Penn State Nittany Lions football team was coached by Joe Paterno in his eighteenth year. The team achieved an 8-4-1 record with an Aloha Bowl game victory over Washington. Even with four regular season losses, the Lions were ranked at #17 in the Coach's poll. Clearly after a national championship it is safe to call 1983 a rebuilding year for Penn State. New players equal a new team.

1984 Penn State Football Season Coach Joe Paterno

The 1984 Penn State Nittany Lions football team was coached by Joe Paterno in his nineteenth year at age 56. With a 6-5 record this can be called a rebuilding year to a rebuilding year. Lots of losses.

1985 Penn State Football Season Coach Joe Paterno Almost Championship

The 1985 Penn State Nittany Lions football team was coached by Joe Paterno for the twentieth year and played its home games in Beaver Stadium in University Park, Pennsylvania. You may recall in the 1983 summary, I suggested that the season was 8-4-1 because of rebuilding, and then with a 6-5 season in 1984 I admitted that the rebuilding needed rebuilding. Along the way, noticing that an Alabama team lost four games after beating Penn State, I realized that nothing is certain in college football. But, Joe Paterno knew how to win. That was certain and in 1985, he showed it again on his way to 1986. This year's 11-1 record was championship caliber.

On November 16, a new regular, Notre Dame, then an unranked opponent, played the #1 ranked Penn State at Beaver Stadium W (36-6).

In the Beaver Stadium historical annals, no game ever had been played in such drenching, cold rain. The heavy rain started Friday night and did not let up until the game was long over. Despite regional TV able to take the fans out of the inclement weather, over 84,000 fans showed up. They expected to see a close game but watched as the top ranked Nittany Lions annihilated Notre Dame en route to an 11-0 regular season and berth in the national championship game vs. Oklahoma in the Orange Bowl.

On November 16, an undefeated PSU team beat Pitt at Pitt W (31-0). PSU was ranked #1 at 11-0 undefeated and were invited to play Oklahoma in the Orange Bowl.

Bowl Game Destroys Undefeated Season

The game was about five or six weeks after the team was in shape and had their last taste of a real football game. Miami had the same circumstances so there are no excuses but PSU had obviously lost its edge. On January 1, 1986, # 1 PSU played #3 Oklahoma in the Miami Orange Bowl and lost the game to a Sooners team that played better than Penn State L (10–25). 74,148 saw the game on the field and NBC showed the game to the willing in the rest of the country. It was a great season, 11-1 with a #3 finish in both the Coach's and the AP polls. Watch out for the next year.

1986 Penn State Football Season Coach Joe Paterno

The 1986 Penn State Nittany Lions football team was coached by Joe Paterno for the twenty-first year. Penn State defeated the Miami Hurricanes 14–10 in the 1987 Fiesta Bowl to win Paterno's second consensus national championship. Joe Paterno knew how to win football games.

On September 6, Penn State opened up this successful season at home against Temple. Temple had been having problems winning against PSU for some years and in fact it still does and this year was no different. #6 ranked Penn State won its home opener W (45-15). Boston College moved its September 20 game from Alumni Stadium to Foxborough to play a tough #5 ranked PSU team.

The Eagles played a close game but lost to the Nittany Lions W (26-14). East Carolina lost at Beaver Stadium on September 27 against a #7 ranked PSU squad W (42-7). PSU had a knack of scheduling its easier games in the beginning to get the team accustomed to the routine before engaging tough game. PSU defeated Rutgers at Beaver Stadium next on October 4, W (31-6).

Cincinnati brought its football team to play #5 ranked PSU at Beaver Stadium on October 11. It was a close game but the Nittany Lions won W (23-17). On October 18, Syracuse played PSU at Beaver

Stadium and were defeated easily by the #6 Nittany Lions W (42-3). A tough Alabama team waited for game seven when PSU was 100% ready for the Crimson Tide.

The PSU squad made quick work of the vaunted Alabama team at Tuscaloosa W (23-3). At 7-0, with the Alabama game behind them PSU moved up in the rankings to #2 in the country. On November 1, PSU traveled to Mountaineer Stadium to play a fine West Virginia team and beat the Mountaineers W (19-0)

On November 8, #2 ranked Penn State played Maryland at Beaver Stadium and won a very, very close match W (17-15). A loss would have virtually ended PSU's championship dreams. Playing the unranked Fighting Irish at Notre Dame Stadium on November 15, it was expected to be close and it was but the #3 ranked 9-0 Nittany Lions prevailed W (24-19).

At 10-0, ranked # 2 on November 22, PSU needed just one more win v Pittsburgh at home to have a perfect regular season. The Nittany Lions got that win W (34-14) before 85,722, and also got a shot at winning the national title in the Fiesta Bowl v #1 ranked Miami.

PSU clinched a spot in the national championship game by beating arch rival Pitt. That it was Pitt made this an extremely gratifying moment. The bitterness of the long-time rivalry emerged with five fist fights, a number of late hits and four offsetting penalties for unsportsmanlike conduct. Many who watched every moment of the game, still enjoy the image of Joe Paterno running across the field late in the game to help break up a scuffle in front of the Pitt bench. They say that was a lifetime priceless moment.

A game marred by fighting!

Rob Biertempfel of the PSU Collegian Student Newspaper wrote about a "game marred by fighting. Here is how he saw the contest:

The Collegian Nov 24, 1986

Game marred by fighting

A funny thing happened Saturday afternoon in Beaver Stadium. They started playing football and a hockey game broke out.

The 86th gridiron clash between the Penn State Nittany Lions and Pitt Panthers was at times more like a boxing match than a football contest, as proved by five fights, three ejections, seven personal fouls and 77 yards in penalties. At one point, late in the fourth quarter, Lion Head Coach Joe Paterno sprinted across the field to help break up a scuffle near the Pitt bench.

The image of Paterno running into a fight may have brought comparisons with Maryland Head Coach Bobby Ross' incident with a referee a few weeks ago, but this situation was different.

The scoreboard showed 4:26 remaining and Penn State ahead 34-14 when Pitt's Teryl Austin returned a punt to the Panthers' 18-yard line. After he was run out of bounds, he flipped the ball into the facemask of Penn State's Brian Chizmar. Five Lions came to Chizmar's defense and the melee was on.

"The next thing I knew I was surrounded," Austin explained afterwards. "Everyone got into it."

The Pitt bench emptied, Penn State players rushed onto the grass and Paterno angrily ran into the fight. Television microphones picked up the coach calling the fighting players a disgrace to the game as he tried to separate them. When the mud had settled, the Lions were assessed a 15-yard personal foul penalty.

Paterno was livid at the referees all day for doing what he thought was an inadequate job. After the game, he explained his anger.

"I thought the officials started wrong when they started with a personal foul here and a personal foul there," he said. "That means nothing and I think the game got a little out of hand. I'm going to sit down and tell my kids not to talk about it because I don't think it's good for football when you play in games like that.

"I've never been in a football game with Pitt when we had so much of that kind of stuff."

Pitt Head Coach Mike Gottfried, who got his first taste of the Penn State-Pitt rivalry Saturday, was much more direct in his comments.

"I'm not going to let an hour go by the rest of next year without remembering what they (Penn State) did," he grumbled after the game in a voice deadened by yelling. "I'm never going to forget what their coach did to me on that sideline, and how their fans embarrassed us."

The game's first confrontation came after Penn State's D.J. Dozier had sliced through the Panther defense for a 26-yard touchdown and a 17-7 Lion lead. As Dozier slowed down in the end zone, Panther cornerback Quinton Jones gave the senior tailback some assistance off the field with a slap and shove. Center Keith Radecic stood up to Jones and was joined by quarterback John Shaffer. The fight that ensued resulted in offsetting personal fouls which enraged the partisan crowd and Paterno, who responded by screaming at the officials.

Penn State cornerback Duffy Cobbs said that Paterno's vocal reaction surprised the team.

"Usually he's the one who tries to calm us down," he said. "When I saw him, I said, 'Anything goes now.' "

Radecic agreed, but noted that the afternoon saw more than its share of intensity.

"He did some things today that were a little uncharacteristic, but I think we all did," he said. "I think we all lost our poise a little bit. There were definitely too many personal fouls and unsportsmanlike contact calls. In the heat of the game you never know what will happen."

The rest of the game had its share of scuffles, taunts and shoves, and at least three players were ejected from the game. Pitt lost linebacker Jerry Wall and wide receiver Bill Osborn. Wall identified linebacker Don Graham as the Penn State player thrown out.

The players themselves seemed to take the fierce play in stride, saying that the nature of the rivalry caused spirited play to turn into violence.

Pitt's Steve Apke, who scuffled with former high school teammate Shaffer in the second quarter after Dozier's touchdown, said the game was out of the referees' hands.

"The refs tried to keep it under control, but things like that are going to happen," the senior linebacker said. "It's a big rivalry; that's just playing hard. When the score starts getting out of hand, people start getting frustrated."

Penn State's Bob White also tried to shrug off the scuffles.

"I think that in a lot of ways that's kind of expected," the senior defensive lineman said. "That's the nature of the game over the years. Things did get out of hand out there for a while. But when you've got a bunch of guys that are going at each other the way we were going at each other; those things are going to happen."

1986 Fiesta Bowl Game

Taking advantage of the long New Year's weekend, this January 2, 1987 encounter was scheduled for Friday. It was another game of the century with #1 Miami coached by Jimmy Johnson, the coach everybody loved to hate, and Joe Paterno, a great winning coach at the helm for the #2 ranked Penn State. The Fiesta Bowl game was played in Sun Devil Stadium in Tempe, AZ (Fiesta Bowl). It was televised by NBC and watched on the field by 74,098. PSU won the game W 14–10 and the national championship.

Shane Conlan A Great Hall of Fame Player

By Dustin Hockensmith | dhockensmith@pennlive.com
on May 22, 2014 at 1:58 PM, updated May 22, 2014 at 2:45 PM

Former Penn State linebacker Shane Conlan was one of 16 inductees into the 2014 College Football Hall of Fame. One of three Nittany Lions on the ballot, Conlan made the cut as a two-time All-American who helped lead Penn State to an undefeated record and the 1986 national championship. Running back D.J. Dozier and offensive lineman Steve Wisniewski also made the final vote.

Conlan thanked late legendary coach Joe Paterno and former defensive coordinator Tom Bradley in his acceptance speech. He added that the Nittany Lions were the only program to offer him a scholarship as a three-sport athlete from Frewsburg High School in upstate New York.

"It's been a tough time last few years at Penn State," Conlan said, beginning to choke up. "So, most of all I want to thank two people that are most important to me in my life, one being the late, great Joe Paterno. Thank you so much for all you've done. We miss you, Coach. And my defensive coordinator Tom Bradley, who found me at a very small school. I had no offers except for one, Penn State, and he went to bat for me."

Penn State linebackers Trey Bauer (35) and Shane Conlan (31) pat each other on the back as Miami's Aoatoa Polamalu watches following Conlan's fourth quarter interception in the Fiesta Bowl, Friday, Jan. 3, 1987, Tempe, Ariz. Penn State defeated Miami 14-10. (AP Photo/Jim Gerberich)

"The Penn State football family is ecstatic that Shane Conlan has been selected for induction into the College Football Hall of Fame," Penn State coach James Franklin said. "Shane is one of the primary reasons why so many people know about the unrivaled tradition of Linebacker U. Shane was a fierce, tough competitor and leader and we are excited that he is being appropriately recognized for his outstanding career with his enshrinement in the Hall of Fame."

Conlan was part of a class that combined inductees from all levels of college football in one class, the National Football Foundation said in a press release. He was one of three linebackers inducted, along with late Alabama star Derrick Thomas and Maine's John Huard.

1987 Penn State Football Season Coach Joe Paterno

The 1987 Penn State Nittany Lions football team was coached by Joe Paterno in his 22nd year as head coach. The team's aggregate record including its Citrus Bowl major loss to Clemson L (10-35) was 8-4 and after a #1 finish in 1986, PSU finished out of the top 20 at #22 in 1987.

1988 Penn State Football Season Coach Joe Paterno

The 1988 Penn State Nittany Lions football team was coached by Joe Paterno in his 23rd season. With a 5-6 record, this is the first losing season in Joe Paterno's first 23 years. A double rebuilding process was underway. PSU was unranked and the team did not qualify for a bowl bid.

1989 Penn State Football Season Coach Joe Paterno

The 1989 Penn State Nittany Lions football team was coached by Joe Paterno in his 24th season. At 8-3-1, the team made a great comeback from the 5-6 record of 1988. Additionally, the Lions were #14 in the Coach's poll and #15 in the AP poll. Moreover, they played and beat BYU in the Holiday Bowl W (50-39).

1990 Penn State Football Season Coach Joe Paterno

The 1990 Penn State Nittany Lions football team was coached by Joe Paterno in his twenty-fifth season. The team had a great 9-2 record. Without the early almost-wins in the first two games of the season, Penn State would have been playing for another national championship. Not this year, however.

1991 Penn State Football Season Coach Joe Paterno "Almost" Championship

The 1991 Penn State Nittany Lions football team was coached by Joe Paterno in his 26th season. They won 11 games including the Fiesta Bowl W (42-17 v Tennessee.) Their two losses were at unranked USC on September 14 L (10-21) and against #2 ranked Miami in Florida L (20-26) on October 12.

#7 PSU was invited and accepted play in the Kickoff Classic on August 29 v #8 ranked Georgia Tech at Giants Stadium. PSU triumphed W (34-22).

1992 Penn State Football Season Coach Joe Paterno

The 1992 Penn State Nittany Lions football team was coached by Joe Paterno in his 27th season. After three great years, 8-3-1, 9-3, and 11-2, one could almost expect a rebuilding year. This year's 7-5 record was a winning season but it was not a contender season as the past three. No championship.

Blockbuster Bowl

PSU accepted an invitation to the Blockbuster bowl with a 7-4 season. The game was played January 1, 1993 at Joe Robbie Stadium in Miami Gardens, Florida. #13 Stanford was hoping to make quick work of #21 Penn State. It was not quick and the game was tough but PSU was beat fairly that day by a Stanford team that had come ready to play ball L (3-24).

1993 Penn State Football Season Coach Joe Paterno

The 1993 Penn State Nittany Lions football team was coached by Joe Paterno in his twenty-eighth year. Joe Paterno figured it was time to stop his run as an independent and begin playing Big Ten teams more regularly. So, PSU joined the Big Ten Conference in 1990 and began play in 1993.

Penn State then won its first Big Ten championship in 1994, and the Nittany Lions won two more in 2005 and 2008. As a deep Penn State fan all my life, after reviewing his life in his football record, I cannot believe what a great coach Joe Paterno was. The mold from which he was cut created the greatest football coaches of all time.

At the end of the 1993 season, PSU was ranked #7 in the Coach's poll and # 8 in the AP with a 10–2 record (6–2 in Big Ten play). The complexion of the PSU schedule would change forever as a result of its playing in the Big Ten Conference. The same-ole same-oles were no longer on the schedule but the schedule was always exciting.

On the road on November 27, #14 PSU beat #25 Michigan State at Spartan Stadium in East Lansing MI W (38-37). This was as close a game as it gets. This game set the stage for the 1994 undefeated season and put out a fair warning that Penn State was for real.

Season ends w/ great game v Michigan State

As we have been touting in this book from way back when PSU won its first game in 1881, the Nittany Lions dominated college football as an independent for over 110 years before the university joined the Big Ten in 1993.

Fast forwarding to recent history as a few of us remember the 1990's. The Nittany Lions had won six bowl games from 1980-89, including three Fiesta Bowls and one Sugar Bowl. Penn State had finished in the AP Top Ten seven-times just in the 1970's, five-times in the 1980's, and already twice in the 1990's plus the team brought in national championships. This was a team that transcended graduating classes. Through its great coaches and players, PSU always knew how to win and when Joe Paterno began his legacy after Rip Engle gave him the keys, Penn State further upped the ante. Just try to beat the Nittany Lions!

PSU won the National Championship again as everybody knows in 1994. But, because we are kind to our opponents, we just whisper about this triumph.

You see, the vaunted 1994 team was not awarded the big prize after a 12-0, undefeated, untied season. It was because the coach chose not to embarrass Indiana and the Hoosiers made the score closer than the game ever was. It was as if the football establishment was waiting to deny Penn State's possible best team ever, the national championship.

Paterno's teams had recorded great seasons before 1994 with a 37-12 record leading up to the great 1994 season in which nothing went wrong in games but the afterthoughts were mostly sour.

1993, the year in which we now find ourselves, was also a great effort and a great result though often overshadowed by the undefeated 1994 team. The pundits say that the final game of that season against Michigan State, the game we have been discussing, set the tone for the run to the top in '94. Penn State showed its mettle and the future looked bright. Nobody could deny a great Penn State Team the Championship in 1994. All PSU had to do was win, win, and win again, and our great University did exactly that. But, we spend enough time on that when we cover 1994 so let's continue with the 1993 season.

In 1993, Penn State was the new guy on the block in the Big Ten. The well talented but less experienced than talented Lions opened a great season with five back-to-back wins. Eventually, the team met Michigan and Ohio State consecutively and these opponents were a measurable cut above the five prior teams. Penn State was not intimidated at all.

The Lions competed with Michigan well for the first three quarters, but the Wolverines kept Ki-Jana Carter from the goal line in the opening play of the fourth quarter. It was hard to take, I regret to say that it sure seemed to take the oomph out of the PSU attack. Officially, the game ended when Kerry Collins threw a rare interception within the last minute of the game, but it seemed to end with Carter's almost TD.

Ohio State gave the Nittany Lions their second loss at Ohio Stadium just two weeks later. PSU had been 6-2 against Ohio State before this encounter but the last time was when they played the Buckeyes in the 1980 Fiesta Bowl. The Nittany Lions back then crushed OSU but the Buckeyes had improved for sure and they were ready for vindication against the Lions.

They got their day. The Buckeyes held Penn State to just two field goals and Kerry Collins was intercepted multiple times. The cylinders were not firing right on O or D. Ohio State finished the '93 season with just one loss. Tough players in 1993 were ready to play but with one year under their belts, they knew better how to get the job done. Fans such as me often forget that most players are between 17 and 23 years old. Some of us have kids that are way older than that!

Despite these two consecutive losses, in 1993 Penn State came back strongly and won-out the rest of their season. It was not a cake-walk.

Michigan State Game

The season topping game was their close win in East Lansing, where they squeaked out the win against a stubborn Michigan State to take home the legendary Land Grant Trophy.

The Big Ten was really on to something when they designated Penn State and Michigan State as rivals, meaning they would duel it out annually to prove which land-grant school was bigger and tougher and of course, badder than the other.

This great game is worth discussing. Michigan State was ranked #25, and Penn State was sitting at the number #14 spot. Neither team was a contender. However, as we know, the honor is everything in college football.

On game day, the field of play was a disaster, and the team play on both sides of the colors reflected that. Michigan State nonetheless broke out of the pack with a 13-0 lead early on. Soon, Joe Paterno would send Mike Archie right up the middle (in true Paterno form) to put some points on the board.

Michigan State wasted no time to respond with another seven points, and this is pretty much how this game went for the rest of the second quarter. By halftime Penn State had slimmed that difference to a one-score deficit, 23-17. The Nittany Lions were just down by 6, and they seemed confident in their stride.

The Spartans turned to their strong passing game in the third quarter, and they increased their lead to 37-17. Some were asking, "Is the Nittany Lions' recent winning streak over?."

All of a sudden, or so it seemed, the Lions were alive and roaring again: Collins completed a 40-yard pass to Bobby Engram, and Penn State was ready to control the game. They got even more when the reliable Linebacker U defense recovered a fumble on Michigan State's 38. Collins drove the Nittany Lions down the field again, and with a Brian O'Neal touchdown, he made it a one score game.

The defense took over and forced a three and out, and gave the ball back to the PSU offense on its own 48. Collins faked a handoff and lofted a beautiful 52-yard pass to Engram (that's three touchdowns in about four minutes, if like me, you are keeping track).

The Spartan offense was inert for the remaining ten minutes and the PSU D helped the team big time to take that Land-Grant Trophy back to Happy Valley. It was a good year for Happy Valley as The Nittany Lions finished their first Big Ten season at the number three spot in the conference.

After the win in East Lansing in 1993, Penn State didn't lose a game until late September 1995. Yes, folks, that means there were no losses in 1994—not a one. You'll read about it next.

1993-1994 Citrus Bowl

Penn State had a great 9-2 record going into the Bowl Season. The Lions were invited to the Citrus Bowl in Orlando Florida on January 1, 1994 at 1:00 PM (prime time New Year's Day) to play #6 Tennessee.

Penn State would not be denied the victory over this substantially higher ranked opponent W (31-13) before 72,456 plus the nationwide ABC TV audience. Nobody was more thrilled than I. Despite the outcome, it did not look good at first as the game began.

Tennessee got off to a great start at were ahead 10-0 after a quick 46-yard field goal and a 19-yard TD pass from Shuler to Cory Fleming.

There were 72,000 singing Rocky Top and that was Rnot the Nittany Lions favorite tune. At 10-0 but very early, it appeared the Vols might take it to the Lions with a big rout.

But with Kerry Collins calling the signals and Bobby Engram catching the pigskin when thrown to him, the Nittany Lions were about to roar. On second down from their own 36-yard line, Collins hit Engram on a wide receiver screen over the middle. Engram picked up a block and outran the defenders down to the Tennessee 29-yard line.

After the game, Engram had no problem noting: "That play set the tone...They saw we had some speed after all, and you could just see it in their eyes they weren't sure they could stop us." It was not long before PSU scored on a 3-yard TD run by Carter, who had been sitting out with a knee injury since the Illinois game. Carter was ready.

Tennessee came right back with an impressive drive down to the PSU 28-yard line where linebacker Tyoka Jackson got a tip on the ball in the air, and safety Lee Rubin intercepted it for the Lions at the 13-yard line. This was as close as Tennessee would come to the goal line for the rest of the day. The rout was on but it was not as originally thought. Penn State got hot and The Volunteers were cold.

Before the break-away, Craig Fayak hit a field goal to tie the game and UT responded with a 50-yarder of their own to take a 13-10 lead. With 1:08 to go in the half, Collins moved the ball down the field with a 12-yard draw play to Mike Archi. He then tossed an eighteen yarder to Engram. With 10 seconds to go at the UT 14-yard line, Penn State called their final timeout. Everyone expected Joe Paterno to elect for the field goal, but to their amazement the offense went back out on the field.

Tennessee sat back in pass defense expecting the Lions to take a shot at the end zone, but Paterno called a draw play to Carter instead. Carter broke a tackle at the line and sprinted into the end zone to give the Nittany Lions a 17-13 lead at halftime. The pundits felt that PSU had sent this message to the Volunteers with this play: "We can do anything we want to do, and there is nothing you can do to stop it."

Joe Paterno let it out at half time in the locker room: "Who do they think they are, telling us they need a better opponent,"

Paterno yelled out to a fully-tuned in team of Nittany Lions: "I'm tired of this Orange team! I'm tired of this Orange Stadium! I'm tired of seeing Orange! Let's go out there and kick the Orange out of them!" Coaches inspire teams.

Penn State did exactly that. The Lions took the second half kickoff and marched 60 yards, with Collins hitting Brady wide open in the end zone to make it 24-13. Engram later added a 15-yard TD catch, and the defense shut out the Vols. The tough PSU D sacked Shuler four times. The final score was Penn State 31, Tennessee 13.

This was one game that even the players felt the negative hype and it had irritated them. Perhaps it had even inspired them. When it was all over, Kerry Collins let it be known that the Penn State team was irritated by the lack of respect for Penn State in the pregame media coverage.

"We heard all week about Heath Shuler and everybody was underestimating us, "Collins said. "We thought all along that we were the better team. All we had to do was come out and prove it." Paterno himself felt obliged to add: "We never thought Tennessee was better than us."

1994 Penn State Football Season Coach Joe Paterno "~~Almost~~" Championship

The 1994 Penn State Nittany Lions football team was coached by Joe Paterno in his 29th year. Hard as it is to believe Penn State had another perfect record at 12-0. But, again, they were not national champions. Instead, they were bequeathed a # 2 ranking, and thus were denied another national championship.

As time goes by and this season is examined more closely, Penn State has been awarded the National Championship by more organizations than just the AP and the Coaches group. Check this out
For exaple, PSU was declared National Champions by four groups— DeVold, Eck, Matthews, and the New York Times. They were declared co-national champions by FACT, NCF, and Sagarin. The were the Big Ten Champion. They were the Rose Bowl Champion

and they won the prestigious Lambert-Meadownlads Trophy. Their Rose Bowl victory over Oregon was more than convincing at W (38-20). So, yes, Virginia, Penn State was the National Champion in 1994. Let others claim what they may. Penn State had itself a great Championship Season. Amen. So be it! No matter what else you hear.

Life sometimes is not fair. Some say the reason PSU did not win the AP and Coaches' championship is that the Big Ten was not a respectable conference.

I don't buy that. I think there are dominating love-fests by the coaches and the AP and they feel a successful program such as Penn State does not need the benefit of the doubt. They were right to a degree but how about fairness? This is not the first time being cheated for Paterno nor for Penn State.

During the season, just two days after beating Ohio State, 63-14, -- yes, 64-13, Penn State University received 28 first-place votes in the Associated Press media poll and 32 first-place votes in the CNN/USA Today coaches' poll. They should have and did and they played flawless perfect ball the rest of the way.

Yet, somehow, two months later, after winning its final five games, Penn State got just 10 1/2 first-place votes in the AP poll and just eight first-place votes from the coaches. Meanwhile Nebraska got 51 1/2 first-place votes from the writers and 54 firsts from the coaches. What happened?

Nebraska was declared #1 and Penn State got the runner up spot at #2. Nobody could tell Joe Paterno his team wasn't the 1994 national champions.

"Who said we didn't win a championship?" Paterno mused. "(A portion of) the media (and the coaches' panel) said we didn't win a championship. We think we won a championship. We did everything we could and we're going to assume we're champions. And that's not to take anything away from Nebraska.

"But I think this team did everything it could, and it's certainly a national-championship-caliber football team. We're going to assume that, that's all. We're going to treat ourselves as champions. I'm going to treat them as champions. And I know Penn State will treat them as champions."

Whatever Penn State Fans or Nebraska fans or anybody who watches a lot of football thought about the ranking situation, it did not matter. What was clear, however, was that the coaches and media members were too lazy to analyze all of the top teams in depth to help them form a proper conclusion. This surely was a reason to get rid of such a system. It had become a popularity contest.

Reality often does not matter when perception is the deciding factor in any difficulty. The perception at this time in 1994 for those with a sentimental affinity for Nebraska was that Nebraska had beaten Miami by one touchdown in the January 1995 Orange Bowl and that made them automatic national champions. It was as if Richard Nixon had made the proclamation again against Penn State.

This time, rather than president Nixon's exuberance with his buddies at a football game, it was a media-driven perception that negated anything Penn State might have done in the Rose Bowl or anything the Nittany Lions accomplished in their record-setting season.

Find me another team that played the likes of Penn State in a year other than 1994 and I will show you a national champion. It did not matter that Miami, ranked # 3 when they played Nebraska had lost to Washington, a team that had four losses.

Miami in 1994 was not what Miami once was. They were ranked #3. Oregon, Penn State's Rose Bowl foe was not what it once was either. But Miami is perceived as a football giant, while Oregon is looked on as a joke. However, Oregon defeated Washington, a team that had defeated Miami 21-7 but none of the pundits cared that Miami was no longer Miami!

There was no way Penn State could overcome that dichotomy of impressions. Facts were not permitted on the table. To this day, I wish the University would put 1994 on the table as a national championship. The players and the coach earned it but the university went with the establishment.

Neither Penn State nor Nebraska played much of a non-conference schedule. Their conferences were supposed to be tough enough. Their best wins were over Southern California and UCLA, respectively. Who wants to make a bid on the better team USC or UCLA? Was the Big ten a tougher conference in which to excel or was the Big 8?

Which conference, the Big Ten or Big Eight, tasked a team more to excel in order to win? Did any of the coaches or the pundits in the AP after the season ended perform a real look-see? Or, perhaps they merely wanted to write their stories or share their opinions without doing real checking? Any rational analysis would suggest that, top to bottom, the Big Ten was much tougher than the Big 8 – hands down. Yet, it did not matter in the voting, but on mattered in the overall notion of a fair system.

Other than Colorado, which got to pound a beleaguered Notre Dame team in the Fiesta Bowl, the Big Eight was comprised of six stiffs. There was no excellence there.

The Conference's only other bowl teams, Kansas State and Oklahoma, lost their postseason games to Boston College and Brigham Young, respectively, by the combined score of 43-13. So, how good was the Big 8 in 1994 and why were they given so much preference over the Big Ten? Why did the Big Ten conference not fight harder to claim a win for PSU, a new member of their prestigious organization?

Conversely, the other Big Ten bowl teams - Michigan, Illinois, Wisconsin and Ohio State - were 3-1 in their bowls. Ohio State lost to Alabama, 24-17, in the final minute. The other three won their games by the combined score of 88-34. So, how could PSU, the Big Ten Champion, be shut out in 1994 in their finest season by a bunch of blowhards that seemed to like a great coach such as Tom Osborne more than a clear championship team coached by Joe Paterno? Say it ain't so, Joe!

1994 Games of the Season

All-Americans Bobby Engram (left) and Kerry Collins celebrate Penn State's thrilling 31-24 win at Michigan on October 15, 1994 in Penn State's first game in Ann Arbor. Engram and Collins were among five first-team All-Americans that led the Nittany Lions to Big Ten and Rose Bowl titles, becoming the first Big Ten team to finish 12-0.

On September 3 to open the season, #9 PSU played Minnesota at 8:00 PM at the Hubert H. Humphrey Metrodome, Minneapolis. It was not scheduled to be a blowout but it was nonetheless W (56–3).

On September 10 at 3:30 PM, a #8 ranked PSU beat #14 USC, a tough team always, at Beaver Stadium in University Park, PA. USC was never in the game. On September 17, Iowa played #6 PSU at Beaver Stadium W (61–21). Then on September 24, at home, #5 ranked PSU shellacked Rutgers W (55–27) before 95,379.

On October 1, #4 PSU traveled to Franklin Field v Temple W (48–21). On October 15, playing #5 Michigan, a #3 ranked Nittany Lions team had its way with the Wolverines in a tough battle against a powerful Big Ten opponent at Michigan Stadium, Ann Arbor, MI. W (31–24). The attendance was 106,382 in the Big House!

On October 29 at 3:30 PM. Penn State played a powerhouse of a team ranked at #21. Ohio State played the #1 ranked Nittany Lions at Beaver Stadium and in the biggest upset of an Ohio State team ever, Penn State could not hold back in its leathering the Buckeyes on National TV W (63–14). OSU was not a bad team at all but PSU was that good.

It is a sweet enough victory to repeat what happened. Penn State handed Ohio State its worst defeat in 48 years in what remains one of the most satisfying victories ever for Lion fans. The lopsided win by the No. 1 Nittany Lions over the No. 21 Buckeyes was impressive enough to write home about. However, it was not impressive enough to keep Penn State on top of the next AP poll. Penn State went on to win its first Big Ten Championship, becoming the conference's first 12-0 team, but as noted finished No. 2 in the final polls.

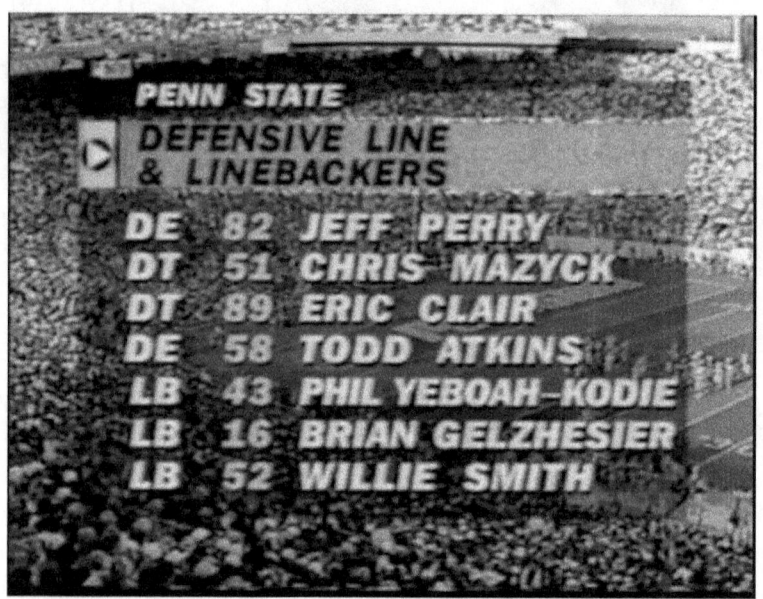

PSU V OSU Oct 29 Right after Game Started

On November 5, somehow PSU was now # 2 in the game v Indiana at Memorial Stadium at Bloomington, IN. It was close but all Penn State W (35–29). Big Ten teams were tough to beat as PSU found out. On November 12 at Memorial Stadium in Champaign, IL, PSU beat the Fighting Illini W (35–31). On November 19, PSU defeated without a doubt the Northwestern Wildcats at home W (45–17)

On November 26, Michigan State came to win at Beaver Stadium v #2 PSU at Beaver Stadium in University Park, PA. The Nittany Lions won decidedly W (59–31) in a high scoring game.

With an 11-0 record, Penn State was ready to win the Rose Bowl on January 2, 1995 to assure itself of a National Championship. The Nittany Lions had beaten every team that it had played and it had one game left, the Rose Bowl

Having won the Big Ten Championship in just its second year and nationally ranked for some reason at # 2 instead of # 1, already declared the Big Ten champion, PSU accepted the Rose Bowl offer to play Pac 10 leader #12 Oregon. Oregon was no worse or no better than Miami at the time but Oregon had three tough losses heading into the Bowl game. When the Rose Bowl was over in Pasadena California, shown on ABC and seen before 102,247 in attendance, Penn State had its way with Oregon W (38-20). Yet, the pundits were not swayed even a little.

This was such a great season, let's talk about it just a little bit more:

1994 Season Recap

On October 23, 2004, Derek Levarse, writing for the PSU Collegian Student Newspaper asked us all to remember a great Paterno season from the past—1994. Penn State went undefeated yet this phenomenal season is not chalked up on any permanent record books as a national championship. In my research for this book, I have found the work of student journalists to be energetic, insightful, and darned interesting. I include this piece here. It would have been even more controversial if we had all read it after the bowl games in January 1995. It is so well written, I wish I had written it myself. Enjoy:

Title: "Remembering the glory days 10 years after Penn State's undefeated 1994 campaign"

The dream was already over, they said. Destiny, taken out of their hands the night before by an undefeated Nebraska team. NBC's Bob Costas had declared the Cornhuskers national champs and the bloom was off the Rose Bowl.

None of it mattered. Jan. 2, 1995, was to be a celebration for Penn State and no one -- not the 'Huskers, the pollsters, nor the Oregon Ducks standing across the line of scrimmage -- was going to stop it.

It's the first offensive play of the game for the Nittany Lions. First-and-10 from the Penn State 17 and Ki-Jana Carter is getting the ball. He has to.

Close your eyes and just listen. You're at home, in the crowd, on the sideline -- it's all the same. The Heisman Trophy runner-up has done this so many times this season that you don't need your eyes to tell you what's happening.

There's still a buzz in the Rose Bowl as Kerry Collins delivers the ball to his tailback. It slows to a murmur as Carter hits a hole that is quickly filled at the line of scrimmage by Ducks cornerback Herman O'Berry.

Then, an explosion.

The murmur becomes a full-fledged shout and you know, somehow, he's done it again. O'Berry is suddenly in the distance as the 5-foot-11 Carter has shed his tackle.

The receivers, Bobby Engram and Freddie Scott, seal off their men and the rest is involuntary. The shout is deafening now. Carter has hit the open field and the blue-and-white partisanship in Pasadena rises to its collective feet.

Oregon's vaunted Gang-Green defense can only watch as he streaks down the field without laying another hand on him.

This was 83 yards, 13 seconds, six points and one undefeated season that a group of guys wouldn't trade for anything in the world.

"I just wanted to get down that field as fast I could to celebrate with him," Engram said, still beaming about the play nearly 10 years later. "That was just an amazing play, coming in the Rose Bowl—that was the game we all grow up watching."

Two years before for Engram and the Lions, the Rose Bowl was the furthest thing from their minds. In 1992, Penn State's final season as an independent, the Lions finished what was then considered a mediocre season at 7-5.

Things would improve considerably for the '93 Lions who capped off a 10-2 season with a 31-13 thrashing of Tennessee in the Citrus Bowl.

But none, save perhaps the guys with no names on their jerseys themselves, could have foreseen the offense that the Lions would unleash upon the nation the following season.

It was Carter at tailback. Engram and Scott as the formidable duo at receiver. Kyle Brady, a 6-foot-6 All-American at tight end who could catch as well as he could block. An offensive line that featured two future long-term NFLers in guards Jeff Hartings and Marco Rivera.

And then there was Collins, the quarterback at the center of it all. This was not the prototypical Joe Paterno quarterback. Todd Blackledge and John Shaffer, whom the Penn State coach had under center for his two national championships, did not have the physical gifts of Collins.

"Obviously the quarterback is the leader, the focal point," Engram said. "Kerry, he's just a guy who made everything click. He made all of the good, tough throws, he was tough in the pocket and he was pretty much the leader."

It was a wealth of talent that came from two of the top-rated draft classes in the country at the time, and it all culminated in a 12-0 season that will forever be known as one of the greatest in school history.

It was a wholly unique experience, even for some of the most talented of the bunch who had never enjoyed the success this team would breed.

Penn State's Kerry Collins—:"Lots more than just a quarterback."

"No, not to that extent," Brady said. "It was brewing around there for years, though. The recruiting class behind mine was No. 1 in the country. And you know, sometimes that stuff doesn't always pan out. But that class turned out to be everything it was advertised as."

But why was it that this skilled group was able to come together? How much of it was pure talent and how much were the Penn State program and the coaching responsible for it?

The '94 team might have been fueled mainly by pure talent, but Brady doesn't think that things are so much different still.

"Like any team, it's all about consistency," Brady said. "There are talented guys on those teams, but it's just a matter of playing consistently, when they have the opportunity, they have to score. And I think that consistency is what's been missing for a few years now."

It's hard now, in the days when 7-5 would be a remarkable finish to the current season, to not wonder how large a gap in talent there is from 10 years ago. It's easy to lay blame on the coaching staff, but it certainly made the tough decisions in the past.

Like navigating around Paterno's self-proclaimed troika of starting running backs -- Carter, Mike Archie and Stephen Pitts.

Paterno stuck with Carter, who answered everyone's questions with a 181-yard, three-touchdown performance in the Lions' opening game rout of Minnesota, 56-3 at the Metrodome.

And the numbers only mounted as the Lions won their next four games by a total of 119 points. All of them were decided by the half, ensuring the starters wouldn't take on the typical wear and tear of Big Ten football as the Lions entered the meat of conference play.

"I got spoiled so bad by that team, we averaged 30-40 points a game," Brady said. "Then I got drafted and played for the Jets and I was like, 'What's going on?' In college, I was out of the game that year by the third quarter every game because we were beating the other team so badly."

Five dustings of inferior teams and a No. 3 ranking meant little, though. Still looking to prove themselves to the Big Ten, the Lions will tell you that there are three games that will forever stick in their minds as the most memorable, all for vastly different reasons.

A date in Ann Arbor with undefeated Michigan, a bizarre afternoon in Illinois and, of course, a trip to Pasadena and a controversy that would help change the face of college football forever.

Time froze and Engram's eyes went wide.

Here it was, right in front of him, coming at an unreasonable speed. Collins had thrown a bullet and it was aimed squarely for him. What took only a few seconds was a moment built up from a year before.

It was the middle of a bye week and 5-0 never felt so precarious. Historically, the Wolverines have had that effect on Penn State.

After all, it was Michigan that spoiled Penn State's Big Ten coming out party in '93 with an infamous goal line stand that helped the Wolverines steal a 21-13 victory in Beaver Stadium, ultimately keeping them from the conference title and the Rose Bowl.

Michigan was ranked No. 7 with a blemish on its record courtesy of a Kordell Stewart 65-yard Hail Mary to Michael Westbrook at the Big House earlier in the season.

This was not a squad to be taken lightly.

Paterno, fully aware of the offensive talent assembled on his squad, would frequently try to get into his players' heads before the season even started in preparation for a game like this. Anything to ready his squad for the rigors of the Big Ten and national gauntlets.

"He really put the hammer down on us as an offense," Brady said. "We as an offense were a lot of older guys, more mature, and we understood what he was doing. We developed a hand signal, where we'd make a circle with our fingers and we'd say, 'Nothing penetrates this circle. Nothing fazes us.' He was trying to put pressure on us like we'd face in a game."

Curiously though, there would be no head games this week. No rigorous practices, no screaming, just a quiet and confident Joe.

And if that didn't make all the difference on the Lions' final sustained drive, when Collins found himself staring down Engram.

Engram had cut inside of Michigan cornerback Chuck Winters, finding himself in single coverage after Archie pulled Winters' deep help by going in motion before the play.

Collins saw it, Engram hauled it in, and the Lions took a 31-24 lead on the Wolverines in the fourth quarter.

"Oh, it was a huge catch," Engram said. "I had a good day but it was an up and down day and we were able to come through and win it. That one's up there pretty high because of the simple fact it was in the last minute and it won the game for us."

History might show that Engram's touchdown grab was the one that silenced the Big House and its then-third highest crowd in college football history of 106,832. But it wasn't the nail in the coffin.

Engram's catch may have been the deciding points, but his memory is perhaps a little off. The score came with 2:53 remaining on the clock and a powerful maize and blue offensive machine needing 80 yards for the tying score.

Wolverine's running back Tyrone Wheatley quickly put the lump back in the throats of Lions fans after the kickoff as he rumbled through several tacklers and reached the 50-yard line.

And then there it was. One of Michigan's two star wideouts, Amani Toomer streaking open past safety Kim Herring as Todd Collins floated the pass to him. Toomer and his counterpart, the speedy Mercury Hayes, had been giving the Lions fits all game long. The future New York Giant Toomer had a knack for big plays and had already torched the Lions seven times for 157 yards and here came what was to be the biggest of them all.

But by some twist of fate, some cosmic force that seemingly watch over Nittany Nation this season, the ball fell just beyond the outstretched hands of Toomer. The would-be score hit the ground with a thud as morose as the groans in Michigan Stadium.

A sigh of relief for most on the visitors' sideline. For most.

"Relieved," Paterno would say after the game, "wouldn't be a word I would use."

Though the defense may have disappointed Paterno on the previous two plays, it came up huge afterwards. Tim Biakabutuka ran just short of the sticks on second down and was then dropped for a loss by linebacker Phil Yeboah-Kodie on third-and-short.

On fourth down just across midfield, Michigan coach Gary Moeller called for a pass. The Lions put pressure on Collins, however, and the pass went toward Hayes.

There was Lions cornerback Brian Miller. Arms outstretched as the ball seemingly fell in between both men.

Somehow, it was Miller who emerged with the football. The Penn State sideline and an entire town in central Pennsylvania erupted.

"Seeing him with the ball and knowing it was finally over," Engram said, his voice trailing as he put his memories and emotions into words. "Knowing it was all done, that all the hard work paid off... it was better than I could have imagined."

The win earned the Lions a No. 1 ranking and an exorcising of demons from the previous year, but not a rest.

Despite a 63-14 homecoming annihilation of Ohio State the following week, a 35-29 win at unranked Indiana that was not as close as the score would indicate, dropped the Lions down to No. 2.

The stage was set for a Saturday that years later, players would simply call, "The Game," culminating (with apologies to John Elway) with "The Drive."

To think it all started with a guarantee.

Not from the undefeated Lions, but from Illinois coach Lou Tepper. The Fighting Illini were boasting one of the top defenses in the country heading into their matchup with Penn State, allowing just 11.3 points a game.

Tepper declared that if his offense could score 28 points against the Lions, his stingy defense would take care of the rest. Loudmouth Illini linebacker Dana Howard had been in this situation before, guaranteeing an upset over Ohio State earlier in the season.

"We haven't let anyone put up those kinds of points and yards and I don't think we will Saturday," Howard said in the week leading up to the game. "If they try to run, we'll smack them in the mouth."

The smack in the mouth came first, not on the field at Memorial Stadium, but the night before the game at the hotel. The one conveniently located next to Illinois' fraternity row. Noise was one thing. Staying on the sixth floor of the hotel, things weren't so bad for the Lions.

Prank calls in the middle of the night were another, especially to Collins' room. Coincidence? Several players at the time wondered aloud, A) how people got the number in the first place and B) how the hotel front desk let the calls go through.

Still, this was nothing entirely bizarre. As far as distracting the opposing team goes in the annals of collegiate pranks, just the calls could be written off for what it was.

But on game day, Saturday morning, the Area 51-esque conspiracy theories were out in full force.

The Lions woke up that day only to discover that the power in the hotel had gone out. What was at first a minor inconvenience -- no television, no lights -- quickly became a disaster that would have been funny, had it not been so tragic.

No electricity means no elevators. Some of the coaches and trainers happened to be placed several floors above the players, making it a long voyage just to get taped up. No electricity means no pregame meal. The large prepared banquet couldn't be cooked.

The end result of things was another hike down to the ground level and a meal that wasn't quite up to the Paterno standard.

"It was crazy," Engram said. "The power went out and the next thing you knew we had to move all of our stuff down and we had to order pizza, subs and chips and stuff. Next thing you know, we're in the game."

Not just in the game, but down 21-0 after a series of mishaps and turnovers on par with the events at the hotel. But the Lions pulled close with a Collins to Scott touchdown off of a fake reverse and would find themselves going into the half down 28-14.

Tepper had his 28 points. Would it be enough?

"The way we felt at halftime ... you know, we just said to the defense, 'Hold those guys and we'll win this game. You hold the score and we'll win this game,' Brady said: "We had so much confidence at half, as opposed to panic, there wasn't any of that. Just a confident assurance."

Confident enough that when they took the field late in the fourth quarter, trailing 31-28 and at their own 4-yard line, there still wasn't any question what the result would be.

"Ninety-six yards, guys," Collins told Engram and Brady in the huddle. "We're gonna go 96 yards."

Ki-Jana Carter breaks away v Illinois in crucial win to undefeated season

Inspired efforts from Collins, Engram, Brady and Carter on a crucial third-and-short at midfield led to this -- an Illini defense with no fight left in it and a handoff to fullback Brian Milne.

For the second time that day, Milne capped off a 95-plus-yard drive with a touchdown plunge. And a 35-31 victory that punched the Lions' ticket to the Rose Bowl.

But as impressive as the 18-point victory over the Ducks would be, it would be equally bittersweet. The dream matchup with Nebraska would never come to pass.

Oh, what could have been?

The postseason is improved these days, though perhaps not enough to the tastes of some on the '94 team. Ten years later and Penn State and Nebraska would have surely played each other for the national title thanks to the BCS system currently in place.

Instead, the Rose Bowl's conference affiliations mandated that the Big Ten champion Lions squared off against the Pac-10 champion Ducks. Meanwhile, the Cornhuskers drew No. 3 Miami in the Orange Bowl and won in dramatic fashion, 24-17. That pedigree was enough to give Tom Osborne's squad the title from both the writers and the coaches.

"Oh man, if only we could have found out," Brady said. "I've joked around with guys on that [Nebraska] team like Zach Wiegert and he's sure they would have knocked our blocks off and I'm sure we would've knocked their blocks off. It's a shame it didn't get to happen. We'd always say we'd meet them in a cornfield in Kansas somewhere just to play them."

Engram agreed.

"We tried everything we could," he said. "We didn't even need it to be televised, we just wanted to play and settle it all. Unfortunately, that wasn't in the plans."

That's pretty much the sentiment of the entire team. The fact that if the '94 season would have occurred 10 years later under the current BCS system doesn't ease the sting much.

Despite changes to the postseason since his collegiate days, Brady is still disgusted with the state of college football in general.

"The whole system is bringing shame upon college football," Brady said. "And I know that sounds like a strong statement, but that's how I feel."

Brady cited the 2000 season, when both Miami and Florida State were 10-1 at the end of the regular season -- the Seminoles' lone loss coming against the Hurricanes -- but Florida State was placed in the title game against undefeated Oklahoma by the BCS system.

"Where's the justice in that?" Brady said. "It's an ugly, ugly fact that it's all about the money and the university and bowl people filling their pockets. And it's so obvious that's what's happening that it discourages me from watching college football games sometimes.

"For the guys that played, pouring their hearts out and it might not happen, their dreams might not happen, just because some white-haired guys in an office are sitting around with smiles on their faces and filling their pockets. And it's at the expense of kids and their dreams."

Despite the still harsh realities of the system, the '94 season did as much to bring about change to college football as anything. It furthered an ageless controversy and ultimately would help bring about change.

Few undefeated teams in history -- whether they won a title or not -- can make that claim.

It's a testament to the team that Penn State isn't able to hold a 10th anniversary celebration for Homecoming against Iowa this weekend. Too many of the guys are still in the NFL.

There are plans for the spring though, a reunion of sorts to be held at April's Blue-White game. For most of the team, especially those still playing, keeping in touch has proven difficult, exchanging pleasantries on the field before games in the pros.

But 12-0 is 12-0.

"I still consider them all my friends, even if we don't stay in touch," Brady said. "This team has a special bond because of that season."

And no amount of time will take that away.

On behalf of myself and all PSU fans, I say PSU was & is #1.

1995 Penn State Football Season Coach Joe Paterno Outback Bowl Win

The 1995 Penn State Nittany Lions football team was coached by Joe Paterno in his thirtieth year as head coach. His PSU Nittany Lions had a great season at 9-3, and their record on the Big Ten was 5-3. It was not a championship but a great year nonetheless.

On November 18 at 12:00 PM, #12 Michigan planned to beat #19 PSU at Beaver Stadium in University Park, PA on ABC TV, yet PSU prevailed before 96,677 W (27–17).

To many football historians who love Beaver Stadium games, this match is simply remembered as "The Snow Bowl." Three days before the game, a surprise 18-inch snowfall made it necessary to use hundreds of paid volunteers to clear the field. But with snow piles all around them, 80,000 freezing fans watched holder Joe Nastasi score a two-yard touchdown off a fake field goal with 2:40 left to secure the Lions' second of three consecutive victories over the tough Michigan Wolverines.

The Snow Bowl v Michigan Pre-Cleanup

Michigan State came so quickly afterwards at Spartan Stadium, after a long ride that the Lions were ready and PSU beat the Spartans W (24-20).

Having such a good year, 8-3, #15 PSU got to play in the Outback Bowl on January 1, 1996   at 11:00 AM v #16 Auburn in Tampa Stadium •at Tampa, FL. Penn State was up for the match and won handily W (43–14 (before 65,313). The Nittany Lions finished 9-3, #12 in the Coach's poll and #12 in the AP. Everybody was looking for 1996

Chapter 18 Joe Paterno Era 1996 to 2011

Coach # 14

Year	Coach	Record	Conf
1996	Joe Paterno	11-2	(6-2 Big 10)
1997	Joe Paterno	9-3	(6-2 Big 10)
1998	Joe Paterno	9-3	(5-3 Big 10)
1999	Joe Paterno	10-3	(5-3 Big 10)
2000	Joe Paterno	5-7	(4-4 Big 10)
2001	Joe Paterno	5-6	(4-4 Big 10)
2002	Joe Paterno	9-4	(5-3 Big 10)
2003	Joe Paterno	3-9	(1-7 Big 10)
2004	Joe Paterno	4-7	(2-6 Big 10)
2005	Joe Paterno	11-1	(7-1 Big 10)
2006	Joe Paterno	9-4	(5-3 Big 10)
2007	Joe Paterno	9-4	(4-4 Big 10)
2008	Joe Paterno	11-2	(7-1 Big 10)
2009	Joe Paterno	11-2	(6-2 Big 10)
2010	Joe Paterno	7-5	(4-3 Big 10)
2011	Joe Paterno	8-1	(5-0 Big 10)
2011	Tom Bradley	1-3	(1-2 Big 10)

JoePa Coached 45 great seasons 1966 to 2010 & part of 2011. This 15-year period, we find some of JoePa's Worst but mostly his best. Nobody could make the team be a contender as well as Joe Paterno!

1996 Penn State Football Season Coach Joe Paterno Fielsta Bowl Win

The overall 1996 record was 11-2, (6-2 in the Big Ten). Their record included a nice win against Texas in the Fiesta Bowl W (38-15). Penn State finished in the top ten in both polls at # 7.

The 1996 Penn State Nittany Lions football team was coached by Joe Paterno in his thirty-first year. Penn STtae had another great winning season with just a few disappointing games.

The 1996 season was also notable as it marked the end of ties in college football, as an overtime system was put into place across all of Division I-A. Penn State's first OT game came in 2000 v Iowa. The 1995 season had overtime rules, but only for postseason games.

The Bowl Alliance was formed to make post-season championships fairer but it did not really work well and over time the current BCS plan was adopted. For example, in 1996, there was a large controversy when #5 BYU was robbed of a spot in a Bowl Alliance game, as they were snubbed in favor of lower ranked teams from Bowl Alliance conferences. Believe it or not Congress got involved.

The Nittany Lions faced off against USC in the Kickoff Classic on August 25 before 77,716 at Giants Stadium in East Rutherford, NJ. PSU won the match W 24-7).

1997 Penn State Football Season Coach Joe Paterno   Citrus Bowl

The 1997 Penn State Nittany Lions football team was coached by Joe Paterno in his 32nd year. Penn State had a respectable season overall at 9-3 (6-2 in the Big Ten). The Nittany Lions were ranked #17 by the Coaches and #16 by the AP. Their season was capped off by being invited to the Citrus Bowl in Orlando but on January 1, 1998, the #11 Lions were beaten in this game by #6 ranked Florida L (6-21).

The home season began on September 6 as #1 ranked PSU defeated Pittsburgh W (34–17) before 97,115. On September 13, PSU beat Temple at home W (52-10). On September 20, still ranked at #1, the Nittany Lions beat Louisville at Cardinal Stadium in Louisville, KY W 57–21. After this convincing win, PSU fell to #2 in the rankings as they prepared to face Illinois in Champagne on October

4. The #2 Nittany Lions beat the Fighting Illini W (41-6) to hold second place.

The real big test of the season was next as a tough Ohio State team came to Beaver Stadium on October 11, and were beaten back by the Lions W (31-27). Now, back at #1, Penn State barely beat Minnesota on October 18 W (16-15). The closeness of this game put PSU in 2nd place as the Nittany Lions played at Northwestern and beat the Wildcats in a tug of war W (30-27).

Still ranked #2 with a 7-0 record, PSU faced #4 Michigan on November 8, and were beaten by the Wolverines L (8-34). Then at #6, on November 15, PSU played #19 Purdue at Ross-Ade Stadium and beat the Boilermakers W (42-7). The Nittany Lions followed this win with another on November 22 at home against #24 Wisconsin W (35-10). Then, it was off to East Lansing, Michigan on November 29 to lose to the unranked Spartans of Michigan State in a blow-out L (14-49).

Not having recovered from the two late-season crippling losses, #11 Penn State lost the Citrus Bowl to # 6 ranked Florida L (6-21).

1998 Penn State Football Season Coach Joe Paterno Outback Bowl Win

The 1998 Penn State Nittany Lions football team was coached by Joe Paterno in his 33rd year. Penn State had another very respectable season overall at 9-3 (5-3 in the Big Ten). The Nittany Lions were ranked #15 by the Coaches and #17 by the AP. Their season was capped off by being invited to the Outback Bowl on January 1, 1999 in Raymond James Stadium in Tampa Florida where they beat #22 Kentucky W (26-14).

On October 31, at Beaver Stadium, the Nittany Lions pitched a shutout against Illinois W (27-0). This game is known for LaVar's leap. If there is one single, memorable but isolated moment frozen in time it was LaVar Arrington's leap over the Illinois offensive line the instant the ball was snapped, tackling the runner in the backfield the millisecond the quarterback gave him the ball. That moment early in the third quarter when the score was already 21-0, had absolutely no impact on the game or the season but it will be forever known as "LaVar's Leap."

LaVar Arrington's Leap was more substance than faith

1999 Penn State Football Season Coach Joe Paterno

The 1999 Penn State Nittany Lions football team was coached by Joe Paterno in his thirty-fourth year. This year the Nittany Lions had a nice 10-3 record (5-3 in the Big Ten), ranked # 11 in both polls. Their record was fine enough for a bowl game and they beat Texas A&M on December 28 in the Alamo Bowl in Texas W (24-0).

LaVar Arrington a Great PSU Linebacker

Penn State Collegian, the Student Newspaper says all that needs to be said about the great football work of LaVar Arrington, one of The Lions best linebackers of all time. There can sure be lots more said as Arrington is one of the greatest Linebackers from PSU. In his write-up in the Collegian author Anthony Picardi got a great perspective on Arrington's football playing days with Penn State University: Enjoy! Being a great linebacker was a big deal at Penn State but the University sure had its share.

Penn State linebacker LaVar Arrington takes a flying leap at Illinois quarterback Kirk Johnson. Collegian File Photo

2000 Penn State Football Season Coach Joe Paterno

The 2000 Penn State Nittany Lions football team's head coach was Joe Paterno. This was another one of those building years (5-7 with 4-4 in the Big Ten). It was just the second losing season for Coach Paterno in his 35-year stint so far at Penn State. Long time defensive coordinator Jerry Sandusky retired before the season began and he was replaced by Defensive coach Tom Bradley.

Penn State, ranked #15 to begin the season agreed to be in the annual Kickoff Classic held at Giants Stadium on August 2th. The Opponent was #22 USC. The Nittany Lions lost the game L (5-29).

2001 Penn State Football Season Coach Joe Paterno

The 2001 Penn State Nittany Lions football team was coached by Joe Paterno in his 36th season with the Lions. Penn State did not play Big Ten teams Minnesota and Purdue this year. Also, due to the events of 9/11, the Virginia game was rescheduled from September 13, 2001, to December 1, 2001.

Much to Nittany Lions Fans chagrin, this would be the second of two-rebuilding seasons. This team had one less loss than the 2000 team, finishing at 5-6 (4-4 in the Big Ten). If you'll look ahead, the agony ends in 2002 as PSU works its way back into the top twenty. But, not this year.

In a Baptism of Fire, The Nittany Lions began the 2001 season on September 1, against a #2 ranked Miami team at home before a home crowd of 109,313 in the newly renovated and expanded Beaver Stadium. Miami came in ready to go and beat the Lions L (7-33).

Adam Taliaferro Rejoices

Those watching while it was happening and after the fact believe that the most emotional and electrifying moment of all-time occurred just before the Miami night game began. It was when Adam Taliaferro walked, then skipped through the south tunnel after suffering a paralyzing injury nearly a year earlier at Ohio State.

This record crowd in and expanded Beaver Stadium that now featured club and private suites gave Taliaferro a long-standing ovation, but the joy ended soon as Miami coasted to victory en route to the national title.

2002 Penn State Football Season Coach Joe Paterno Citrus Bowl

The 2002 Penn State Nittany Lions football team was coached by Joe Paterno in his thirty-seventh year as head coach. The team improved substantially over 2000 and 2001, finishing the full season at 9-4 (5-3 Big Ten) and #15 in the Coach's Poll and #16 in the AP. Ranked #10 at game time, PSU was invited to the Citrus Bowl against #19 Auburn. In a game played on January 1, 2003, in which neither team showed much offense, Penn State scored just four points less than the Tigers and lost the Bowl game in Orlando, FL, L (9-13).

2003 Penn State Football Season Coach Joe Paterno

The 2003 Penn State Nittany Lions football team's head coach was Joe Paterno in his thirty-eighth year. I bet JoePa in reflection would have still coached this year even though it was his worst ever. It was one of the worst seasons in PSU history. I guess if you bring home a lot of big ones, having a season in which there appears to be no harvest is expected. But, Penn State Fans get agitated when the W's are not there in the column. Realistically all home teams feel the same. Our coach is supposed to win. Wins rarely happened in 2003. In a word, the year stunk with a 3-9 record and the second worst record in the Big Ten (1-7). Illinois at 0-8, had to live with its season for some time to come.

2004 Penn State Football Season Coach Joe Paterno Championships

The 2004 Penn State Nittany Lions football team's head coach was Joe Paterno in his thirty-ninth year. The wonderful coach JoePa and the same wonderful man over the last two years has begun to have trouble winning games in his later years of coaching. In 2004, he was 77 years old but still spry and he did have player issues.

If this were a mystery novel you'd have to wait until next years and the next to see how this comes out but it is not. It is real, it is fact based, and if you want to, you can look it up but soon, in the next ten pages or so, you will have all your answers about the Penn State record under Joe Paterno. He stopped coaching in his forty-sixth year and in 2002, it was his thirty-ninth. He was one heck of a coach!

2005 Penn State Football Season Coach Joe Paterno

The 2005 Penn State Nittany Lions football team for the fortieth year in a row were coached by the one and only JoePa (Joe Paterno) in another of many great winning seasons. Just when you think there is a systemic reason for losses that may involve coaching, the same Paterno formula again brings in more wins than anybody could ever expect and guys like me and perhaps you too, regardless of where we were in the dark losing years say, "Of course, that's JoePa. He's our coach."

This was Paterno's toughest mountain to climb. The Nittany Lions were coming off of back-to-back losing seasons, finishing 3-9 in 2003 and 4-7 in 2004, capping a stretch from late 1999 where Minnesota upset the #2 Nittany Lions with a late field goal until the goal line stand at Indiana. There were four of five seasons being losing seasons and the lone winning season in 2002 featuring many extremely frustrating close losses. You lived through the frustration in this book, and this is one of our chances to smile.

This stretch was called "The Dark Years", sometimes including 2002 as well. The team finished the sketchy 2004 season with wins over Indiana and Michigan State. As always, a strong finish helps springboard momentum into the next season (2005 in our case). So here we are with a great year, which we are about to discuss, having closed out 2004 with two nice wins, there was a ton of hope for continuance into the 2005 Nittany Lions season. It happened.

Instead of five starters in 2003, this year's team returned 18 starters from last year's squad. Eight starters returned on offense, led by starting quarterback Michael Robinson who also played at wide receiver, tailback, and punt returner during his first three years at Penn State. Robinson played exclusively under center after the graduation of Zack Mills.

PSU heralded the fact that it had nine defensive starters return from a unit that did not allow more than 21 points in a game in 2004. Also returning was safety Chris Harrell who suffered a neck injury in 2003 and missed the 2004 season. It was time to play.

Michael Robinson, Alan Zemaitis, and Paul Posluszny were elected tri-captains of the football team in 2005. Posluszny was the first junior captain since 1968.

Penn State had made the pundits wary in their last four out of five tough seasons. So, they started the season unranked in both the AP and the Coaches college football preseason polls. Who can argue with an excellent # 3 finish in both polls and an 11-1 overall record as well as a 7-1 record in and co-championship in the Big Ten, Penn State had recovered and the prognosis for the patient was good.

On September 3, PSU began the season and the home season by beating South Florida at Beaver Stadium W (23–13). On September 10, the next week, a tough Cincinnati team was taken down by the Lions at Beaver Stadium in University Park, PA W (42–24). Finally winning, PSU next engaged Central Michigan at home on September 17 W (40–3). Then, on September 24 at Ryan Field in Evanston, IL, PSU defeated a scrappy Northwestern squad W (34–29).

On October 1, the still down by the press but tough on the field degraded Nittany Lions, unranked after four straight wins, played at home against the #18 Minnesota Gophers and showed the stuff from which they were made before 106,604 at Beaver Stadium and ABC TV. PSU won big W (44-14). Somebody had to notice that Penn State was again playing Nittany Lions Football.

Never giving up in the tough games, on October 8, a finally ranked #16 PSU hosted the Ohio State Buckeyes before 109,839 at home and outlasted the Ohio Squad W (17-10).

The Nittany Lions' win over the No. 6 Buckeyes before another frenzied night time "whiteout" crowd of 109,839 was an epic milestone, marking the return of Penn State to the college football elite. The Lions took the lead in the Big Ten Conference and went on to finish No. 3 in the polls with a BCS Orange Bowl win and their best record (11-1) in 11 years.

Ready to play anybody and win, the 2005 Nittany Lions finally met a team that could beat them. Unranked Michigan was a different team at home than away. The Wolverines hosted the game at Michigan Stadium in Ann Arbor, MI (aka, the Big House) before a huge crowd of 111,249. They barely beat Penn State (two-points) L (25-27) but they won nonetheless. This tough Michigan team was the single reason why the Nittany Lions were not undefeated and untied in 2005. In his fortieth year Paterno was still outclassing all coaches as they came by. What a record! Michigan somehow survived Paterno in 2005.

On October 22 at Illinois the #12 PSU Lions won big…very big against the Fighting Illini W (63-10). On October 29, on Homecoming, PSU beat Purdue at home W (33-15). On November 5, another Big Ten Tough team, Wisconsin were beaten by #10 Penn State at home W (35-14) before 109,865 electrified PSU fans and maybe a few others. On November 19, PSU took out its Michigan frustration against a guiltless Michigan State at Spartan Stadium in East Lansing, MI with a convincing win W (31–22).

At 11-1, On January 3, 2006 at 8:00 PM, #3 ranked Penn State won a shot at the Orange Bowl against nemesis #22 Florida State at Dolphin Stadium in Miami Gardens, FL (aka the Orange Bowl). After winning the opportunity to play during the season. PSU won the game in three overtime periods W (26-23). Bravo PSU!

2006 Penn State Football Season Coach Joe Paterno

The 2006 Penn State Nittany Lions football team's head coach was Joe Paterno in his forty-first year. As always, the Lions played home games at Beaver Stadium in University Park, Pennsylvania. Though not as clean as 2005, PSU was making everybody take notice again with a season record of 9-4 (5-3 in the Big Ten). PSU had a winning sason in the Big Ten and against non-Big-Ten teams. Certainly, there were better years but this signaled an escape from the Dark Years back into the top 25 with a Coaches ranking of 25 and an AP rank of 24.

The 2006 season began with the Nittany Lions ranked #19 in the AP and Coaches preseason polls. With losses to Notre Dame and Ohio

State, the team dropped out of the rankings, but snuck back into the top 25 at season end.

Everybody had been looking for an unprecedented 2006 after Penn State had some major unexpected success in 2005 after two consecutive losing seasons. The 2005 team was a big part of the 2006 team. As you recall from last year's synopsis in this book. The team began 2005 unranked in any poll, and yet finished 11–1 and ranked third.

Paul Posluszny and Levi Brown were elected co-captains of the football team for 2006. Posluszny became the team's first two-time captain since 1969. No matter which PSU game you watched in 2005 or 2006, you would hear Posluzny's name accoladed for his fine play.

In 2006, Pozlusny kept at his excellence and was also named the 2006 Big Ten and consensus national pre-season Defensive Player of the Year. The Nittany Lions team was ranked No. 19 in both the AP and Coaches college football preseason polls. They made the top 25 and came close to an even better season.

Before we go on with the games of the season, let's profiled Paul Posluzny as this was his senior year. Posluzny was one of the greatest linebackers in the greatest Linebacker school in the country, Linebacker U, aka PSU.

Great Player: Paul Posluzny,

In 2005, Paul Posluszny was a junior outside linebacker at Linebacker U and captain for Penn State. He had a great year as a junior with 82 tackles, ranking third in the Big Ten and 11th in the nation with 11.7 tackles per game. In 2005 and 2006, Posluszny was named a semifinalist for the 36th Rotary Lombardi Award, presented to the nation's top lineman or linebacker. In both years, the 6-2, 234-pound linebacker was one of 12 semifinalists up for the prestigious award and in 2005, he was one of only three non-seniors chosen. On November 15, 2005 Posluszny was selected a finalist.

He was joined as a finalist by Louisville defensive end Elvis Dumervil, Ohio State linebacker A.J. Hawk and Texas defensive tackle Rod Wright. Ohio State's A.J. Hawk won the award but Paul

Posluzny, just a junior in 2005, competing for the award by playing his brand of football, had turned a lot of heads. The award is presented to the nation's top lineman or linebacker.

In the football version of the never-ending story, Penn State All-American Paul Posluszny, who did cleanly win the prestigious 2005 Butkus Award as a junior, was again selected a finalist for the 2006 honor, which is presented to the nation's top linebacker. A fellow Big-Ten player, LaMarr Woodley from Michigan was selected out of the top four. Clearly Posluzny's nomination as a finalist shows how toughness and the abilities of this great football player. As a new guy to sports journalism, I find it quite strange however that a school that has put out the best cadre of linebackers in America has had such a hard time having many of them gain this award.

In 1978, Bruce Clark received the award and then during a period in which PSU had many top linebackers, none made the cut until Carl Nassib got the award in 2015. Just saying! OK, I am saying even more. Would anybody off the street believe than Clark and Nassib were not linebackers? And, so Linebacker U has never won the award with a linebacker. Strange! Strange like all the undefeated season without a championship. OK, enough jawboning.

Posluzny started playing when he was six, back home in the Pittsburgh area. He recalls his dad asking if he wanted to do something new and play football. So, he said sure and gave it a shot. He's been playing ever since. Paul Posluzny had a great high school career, was highly recruited, and he felt really comfortable coming to Penn State. He likes to say that one of his favorite notions about Penn State is that it is Linebacker U and he is a linebacker. He feels that anytime you play a position like linebacker at a school known for that, it's really an honor and a privilege. To Posluzny, it is something to try to uphold.

Baseball is his favorite other sport. Like many of us who are not seven-foot-tall, he once liked basketball. His major at PUS is finance, but he is not exactly sure how he picked it. Posluzny will need that finance degree in life to take care of his holding from being a star professional athlete.

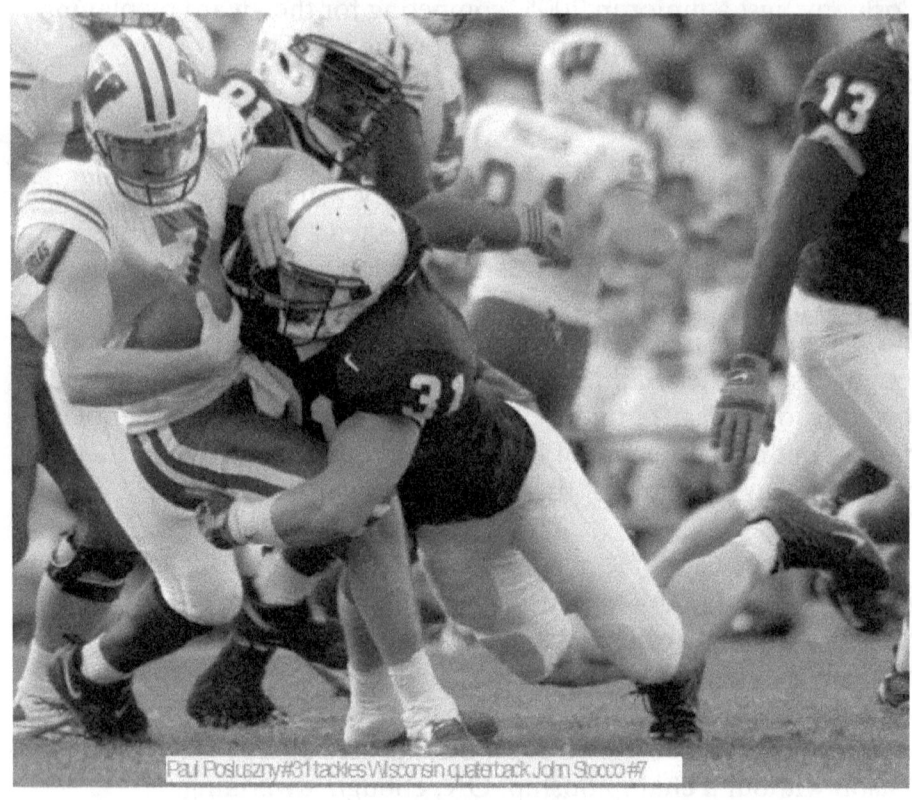

Paul Posluszny #31 tackles Wisconsin quaterback John Stocco #7

Posluszny became just the second two-time winner of the Chuck Bednarik Award, presented to the nation's top defensive player, in 2006. In 2005, he also won the Butkus Award, presented to the nation's top linebacker and was a finalist for the '06 honor.

He was the 13th Nittany Lion to be named a two-time first-team All-American, Posluszny also was a two-time finalist for the Rotary Lombardi Award.

He was selected Big Ten Defensive Player-of-the-Week a conference-record five times in his career. He served as The Nittany Lions' first two-time team captain since 1968-69. He set the record for Penn State career tackles with 372.

He was a starter in his last 37 games at PSU. He became the first Nittany Lion to lead the team in tackles three times and to post three 100-tackle seasons, recording 116 in 2006. Posluszny also was a two-time first-team ESPN--The Magazine Academic All-American, and was selected the 2006 Academic All-American-of-the-Year among Division I football players.

Posluzny has only good things to say about Joe Paterno: *"He teaches us about really just growing up and being a man,"* POZ once said. *"Besides the football, he's preparing us to be good men in life."*

He and Jeff Hartings (1994-95) are the only Nittany Lions to earn first-team All-America and Academic All-America honors twice. Posluszny graduated with a degree in finance in 3 1/2 years and was selected by the Buffalo Bills with the second pick of the second round in the 2007 NFL Draft. He was later signed by Jacksonville as an unrestricted free agent on July 29, 2011.

As a Pro, this great LB started 101 career games and is now in his seventh season with the Jaguars. He has impressive stats with career totals including over 1,079 tackles (764 solo), over 12 INTs, over 12.0 sacks, eight forced fumbles, three fumble recoveries and 32 passes defensed. He was voted to Pro Bowl in 2013.

2007 Penn State Football Season Coach Joe Paterno

The 2007 Penn State Nittany Lions football team was coached by Joe Paterno in his 42nd year and played its home games in Beaver Stadium in University Park, Pennsylvania. Penn State was ranked #17 in the AP and #18 in the Coaches college football preseason polls.

On April 27, 2007, State College police announced that six members of the squad were charged with a range of criminal charges related to an altercation that occurred in an apartment in downtown State College earlier that month. Most of the charges were eventually dismissed or were whittled away by pleas agreements.

For his part, not confining the issue to just six players, Coach Paterno announced that, because of the incident, the entire football team will clean Beaver Stadium on Sundays after home games, a task usually handled by members of Penn State's club sports teams. The team began serving this punishment following their 59–0 victory over Florida International.

The Nittany Lions finished the season with the same record and same ranking as 2006 – 9-4, and #25 and #24 respectively in the two major polls

2008 Penn State Football Season Coach Joe Paterno

The 2008 Penn State Nittany Lions football team was coached by Joe Paterno in his forty-third year. Ranked #6, PSU had a great record of 11-1 going into the Rose Bowl v #5 USC L (24-38). The team finished with a great winning season of 11-2 and were ranked #8 in both polls.

2008 Michigan game

On October 18, The Lions took on a very powerful Michigan team at Beaver Stadium, and were relentless in trouncing the always-tough Wolverines W (46-17).

The crowd went nuts after this long-sought victory. Huge carloads of exhilaration emanated from the first victory over Michigan after nine straight losses over 12 years. This bad record may fade from the mind in the future, but the 110,017 impassioned Homecoming fans thoroughly enjoyed the second half thrashing under the lights as Beaver Stadium rocked and rolled, and PSU picked up a fine W (46-17).

Like many other great PSU games at Beaver Stadium, there were thousands of white pompoms fluttering as 100,000 Penn State fans broke into a sing-along as the happy night fell on Beaver Stadium in the Happy Valley.

Joe Paterno had picked up many nemeses in this 60 years of coaching but they say his greatest nemesis was Michigan and its nasty, victory-seeking Wolverine football team. On this evening in October, these warriors from mid-America were about to be vanquished by a #3 ranked Nittany Lions and its 81-year-old coach. The post-game celebration would create the need for a bird's-eye view of party time in Happy Valley.

Though the season ended without a championship at the time, JoePa was getting a great look at some of the folks in his lineup that were about to make PSU a national championship contender.

Behind the running of Evan Royster and a few momentum-shifting plays by the defense and special teams, the PSU got the game going its way by withstanding the Wolverines' early moves and most importantly, the Nittany Lions worked as hard as they could to not only snap a nine-game losing streak to their Big Ten rivals, they whacked them a good one W (46-17) on this particular Saturday.

Paterno was limping and so he was not on the field to enjoy his record 380th victory. The outstanding master of the college coaching profession was relegated to working from the press box for a third consecutive week because of his sore hip and leg.

"My being upstairs -- it's funny, I'm not sure that's not the best place for a head coach," he said. "I mean you really get a view of things, I get a better view of football games from up there than I ever do on the sideline."

What Coach Paterno saw was a team that should be no worse than third in the BCS standings when it heads to Big Ten rival, and eternal powerhouse Ohio State next week.

"Am I starting to like it up there? I'll never like it, it doesn't mean that the team might be better off with me up there," Paterno said.

No team had ever won as many in a row against Penn State during Paterno's 43 seasons at the helm than Michigan. But if ever there was an opportunity for the Nittany Lions (8-0, 4-0) to break the streak it was 2008. The Wolverines at (2-5, 1-2) were struggling in their first season under coach Rich Rodriguez, but like many teams with new coaches, they expected things to get better as time went by. Nonetheless, they were a powerful team.

"It's a fact, you take it year by year, game by game, we lost to them last year, and coach has made a great point this week, that this Penn State team has not lost to this Michigan team," center A.Q. Shipley said.

Michigan came in the game as a 23 1/2-point underdog because they were not at prime under their new coach Rodriguez, for sure. The Wolverines were unaccustomed to being low in the odds maker's opinions.

Michigan looked like a good bet early with their spread offense clicking as they sped to a 17-7 lead early over Penn State in the second quarter. But the Lions (8-0, 4-0) soon deciphered the spread, and got its own high-powered version of Rodriguez's offense rolling. The lions delivered the knockout punch with a safety, a partially blocked punt and a forced fumble on consecutive second-half Michigan possessions. Michigan did not look good.

"Oh, we executed for a while and then we didn't," said Rodriguez, whose team needs to win four more games to avoid Michigan's first losing season since 1967. "That's what happened. We executed, we moved the ball a little, and when we didn't, we didn't."

Jared Odrick gave Penn State its first lead of the game at 19-17 when he dragged down backup quarterback Nick Sheridan in the end zone with 4:39 left in third quarter.
The free kick set the Nittany Lions up at midfield, Royster's 21-yard run put them at the 1 and Daryll Clark sneaked in at 3:04 to make it 26-17.

Royster, one heck of an athlete, ran for 174 yards on 18 carries, with a 44-yard TD run in the first quarter.

A minute later, Nathan Stupar blocked Zoltan Mesko's punt deep in Michigan territory and Penn State turned the short kick into a Kevin Kelly 32-yard field goal on the first play of the fourth.

60 seconds or so after that, Aaron Maybin sacked Steven Threet, who fumbled, and the Lions took over at the Michigan 19. A sore elbow forced Threet to miss a few series.

Clark's second 1-yard sneak turned the final 12 minutes into a Beaver Stadium celebration bash, with Penn State fans singing along to "Sweet Caroline" and enjoying their team's first victory against Michigan since 1996. It was as Lawrence Welk would say, "Wunnerful!"

The Wolverines had surely tormented Paterno and his Nittany Lions over the prior 12 seasons, with too many lopsided losses and heartbreaking defeats. In 2005, the last time Penn State was in the hunt for a national title, it was Michigan that scored a touchdown on the final play to hand Paterno's team its only loss of the season.

This one couldn't have started better for Michigan but things that start well do not always end well. After a three-and-out for Penn State, Michigan put together its longest drive of the season. The 14-play, 86-yard march featured all the best of Rodriguez's spread offense. The option cleared running lanes for Threet and Brandon Minor, who surpassed his season high on the drive with 42 yards rushing.

Minor finished it off with a 5-yard TD run. "But we've been seeing little glimpses of that all season," Minor said.

A Penn State fumble led to a 27-yard field goal by K.C. Lopata and the Nittany Lions faced their largest deficit of the season.

Sometimes one cannot recognize a comeback until it is mostly finished. After Royster's 44-yard TD romp, Michigan went on the march again.

Another near-flawless drive by the Wolverines, this one 78 yards, was capped by Minor's 1-yard plunge and it was 17-7 early in the second quarter. Minor had 117 yards on 23 carries.

Pundits queried if it were possible that the mere sight of those winged helmets had their team mystified. The vaunted wolverines were ready to win at a moment's notice. But, the notice never came.

Michigan had 185 yards in the first quarter, but only 106 the rest of the way. Penn State's defense can be stacked up against the best in the land and it would win.

"We really stayed calm, we knew Michigan was going to come in and try to play us hard, they do it every year," Royster said. "We just needed to adjust to it."

With just 23 seconds left in the half, the game was being played at top speed. Clark found Jordan Norwood for a 3-yard touchdown pass to make it 17-14, it seemed as if Penn State had come through the worst of it and grabbed control of the game.

The second half would have its rewards for the Nittany Lions as they soundly beat the Wolverines W (46-17). And ain't that sweet!

After Michigan, it seemed nothing could beat the Lions. But, Ohio State was the next on October 25, week and #10 Ohio State always played its best at home and rarely lost to Penn State. Would this game, played at Ohio Stadium, with so much on the line be different? ..... Answer = Yes! This was a different Penn State team.

PSU won this important game W (13-6. Sometimes when a team triumphs over its biggest threat in a season, they relax a bit and the next tough team claims a victory. On November 8 at Iowa, Penn State lost its first game of the season in what would have been an undefeated championship season, to a really tough Iowa Team by just one point L (23-24).

#7 PSU came back on November 15 v Indiana and defeated the Hoosiers at Beaver Stadium W (34-7). On November 22, #17 Michigan State played the Lions at Beaver Stadium. Penn State had fully recovered from the Iowa loss and beat the Spartans in a blowout-shootout W (49-18.

On January 1, 2009, #6 Penn State had another shot at greatness as it took on #5 USC in the Rose Bowl. USC was always tough and this was a special year for the Nittany Lions. The setting was Pasadena California in the Rose Bowl Stadium. The game was televised by ABC and the attendance was 93,293. It was a great game. PSU lost by 12 points in a real determined battle L (24-38) PSU finished the season 11-2. It was a fine # 43 season for Coach Joe Paterno.

2009 Penn State Football Season Coach Joe Paterno

The 2009 Penn State Nittany Lions football team was coached by Joe Paterno in his forty-fourth year. The Nittany Lions continued to play home games in the newly massive Beaver Stadium in University Park, Pennsylvania. As an aside, for those concerned about academics and athletics, in 2009, Penn State University had the highest graduation rate among all of the teams on the Associated Press Top 25 poll with 89% of its 2002 enrollees graduating. Miami and Alabama tied for second place with a graduation rate of 75%.

2009 was also another great year for football, though the two losses were heartbreaking, coaches are paid gazillion dollars a year to achieve records such as PSU's 11-2 record this particular year. Though 82 years of age in the 2009 season, Paterno never weakened.

He was strong and the squad was strong. How can you argue with an 11-2 record? The Nittany Lions also won the Lambert-Meadowlands Trophy award to the best team in the ECAC for the 28th time and the second consecutive year. Penn State is an impressive team and Joe Paterno, even in his few losing seasons, was an impressive coach.

Great Player Sean Lee

Sean Lee was in the on-deck circle at Linebacker U to be the Linebacker Apparent. He had been a three star recruit out of Pittsburgh but he broke into the Paterno lineup early. He made his Penn State debut as a true freshman in the 2005 classic whiteout win over Ohio State. He started every game as a true sophomore, ending the year third on the squad in tackles. He maybe had become a PSU Linebacker as in his junior season in 2007, he finished the year second in the whole Big Ten in tackles, and he was named second team All-Big Ten.

He would have had an even bigger 2008 when an ACL tear in spring practice crippled him while it was repairing after surgery. He sat on the sidelines wearing a head set during the games watching for things to report. Penn Staters were hoping that after such a nurturing Lee would be back at Beaver Stadium in 2009. It was not what it was expected to be. He came back as we knew he would.

2010 Penn State Football Season Coach Joe Paterno Outback Bowl

The Penn State Nittany Lions football team was coached by Joe Paterno in his forty-fifth and last full season with Penn State University. Team captains for the 2010 season were wide receiver Brett Brackett and defensive tackle Ollie Ogbu. After a number of great seasons in a row, especially the outstanding 2009 season, it was again time for some rebuilding. The Nittany Lions finished the season 7–6, with a 4–4 record in the Big Ten play. They qualified and they played in the Outback Bowl where they were defeated by Florida L (37-24). The bottom line is that it was another winning season.

2011 Penn State Football Season Coach Joe Paterno

The 2011 Penn State Nittany Lions football team was coached by Joe Paterno in his forty-sixth and final year. Coach Paterno was the head coach for the first nine games of the year in what looked like it might be another championship season after the rebuilding year. As everybody knows there was a major scandal at Penn State and the Coach was fired in the wake of the devastating allegations involved. JoePa passed away after the season on January 22, 2012. He will go down in historty as one of the most effective coaches in college football history – 409 wins and some regrets.

Defensive coordinator Tom Bradley took over the team for Joe Paterno. Without discussing the merits of the case as this is not a topic in this book, it is certain that the firing of the head coach main stream was very disruptive to the season. The Nittany Lion players continued to work hard and they were clearly innocent victims of the situation and they continued to play but with heavy hearts.

Penn State finished the season 9–4, 6–2 in the Leaders Division of the Big Ten to be co–division champions with Wisconsin. Due to the head-to-head loss to Wisconsin, they did not represent the division in the inaugural Big Ten Championship Game. They were invited to the Ticket City Bowl where under Tom Bradley's best efforts as interim coach, they lost to Houston 14–30.

You may remember that Penn State began the season with an unsettled quarterback situation. There was a battel between sophomore Rob Bolden and one-time walk-on junior Matt McGloin split starting duties in the 2010 season. Rob Bolden was named the starter for the season opener against Indiana State, but things changed.

Matt McGloin was the first walk-on quarterback to start at Penn State since scholarships were reinstated in 1949. Prior to his college career, McGloin was a Pennsylvania all-state quarterback while attending West Scranton High School, a few miles from where I live. He became the starting quarterback for Penn State Nittany Lions football team and led the Lions from 2010 to 2012

The season began like any other on September 3 at Beaver Stadium v Indiana State. #25 ranked PSU defeated the Sycamores W (41-7).

Tom Bradley led the disenchanted PSU Nittany Lions to the Cotton Bowl and PSU lost L (14-30). From the Nebraska game on, nothing seemed real as the whole football program was in disarray.

Chapter 19 Bill O'Brien Era 2012 to 2013

Coach # 15

2012 Bill O'Brien 8-4   (6-2 Big Ten)
2013 Bill O'Brien 7-5   (4-4 Big Ten)

Penn State head coach Bill O'Brien leads his team onto the field at Beaver Stadium for an NCAA college football game against Navy in State College, Pa., ...

2012 Penn State Football Season Coach Bill O'Brien

After over 60 years of coaching at Penn State (15 as assistant and 46 as head coach), Coach Joe Paterno passed away from Lung Cancer on January 22, 2012. His disease was once diagnosed as very treatable. Many of us who admire his work and who admired the man in life and in death believe that the consensus understood that this good man's being fired and not having done enough to help others was more than enough to kill him, or deplete his desire to live, thus hastening his death. I miss him every time I see the blue and white.

So many fans and pundits and alumni who could have simply suggested that they did not buy into his major involvement at all in the scandal, as I would have, stayed silent. Joe Paterno died not a hero as he should have passed out of life. Surely, our merciful Lord has him slotted properly.

Unfortunately, the greatest figure in Penn State Football from the day football was invented, died as a potential reprobate instead of a great hero. That, in my opinion killed him as much as lung cancer from a very treatable disease in January 2012. His fortitude if he felt it was worth it, would have given us the man who could speak about so many great seasons and so many great players, and how to live life.

How did the decisions made by non-football people help PSU or sports in general? These decisions were all off-base and so they did not. It did not.

Unlike the last forty-six years, at the beginning of the 2012 Penn State Nittany Lions football season, the PSU team needed a new coach. It would be Bill O'Brian, a good man. PSU was coached in 2012 by Bill O'Brien, and not Joe Paterno or Tom Bradley. It was O'Brien's, first season and so, as had been the accustomed venue for his team, the Lions played home games in Beaver Stadium in University Park, Pennsylvania, US.

PSU continued as a member of the Big Ten Conference and the team played in the Leaders Division. Due to NCAA sanctions, Penn State was ineligible to play in a bowl game for the 2012 season. The NCAA hurriedly had placed Penn State in the toilet before the verdict had been drawn properly on the 2011 scandal. I wrote a couple books on my feelings of how this all went down. Feel free to review their jackets on my Amazon page amazon.com/author/brianwkelly.

O'Brien was hired as Penn State's 15th head football coach, replacing Hall of Fame coach, Joe Paterno. He was introduced as the head coach at a press conference on January 7, 2012. The team added player names to the back of their jerseys to recognize the players who stayed with the program despite adversity, and they also wore a blue ribbon to support child abuse victims. Football issues were not as important as human issues. PSU was right there offering thoughts of redemption. But, no redemption was to be offered to Joe Paterno despite his contrition. God Almighty will take care of this coach for sure.

After losing its first two games, the Nittany Lions finished their season winning eight of their final 10 to finish with a regular season record of eight wins and four losses (8–4). They were not eligible to participate in a bowl game despite their winning record.

Many PSU fans were wondering why the team and players were suffering as their playing football with encumbrances seemingly positioned to punish the wrong people. The student athletes were punished. The state of Pennsylvania was punished. Coach Paterno was punished unmercifully while there was only one accused

There seems to be those in the media ready to attack great institutions such as the Catholic Church, and Penn State University, while giving a pass to others that they would prefer to protect.

CBS News reports the following:

> *Hofstra University researcher Charol Shakeshaft looked into the problem, and the first thing that came to her mind when Education Week reported on the study were the daily headlines about the Catholic Church.*

"Think the Catholic Church has a problem?" she said. "The physical sexual abuse of students in schools is likely more than 100 times the abuse by priests."

So, in order to better protect children, did media outlets start hounding the worse menace of the school systems, with headlines about a "Nationwide Teacher Molestation Cover-up" and by asking "Are Ed Schools Producing Pedophiles?"

> *No, they didn't. That treatment was reserved for the Catholic Church, [and now Penn State University] while the greater problem in the schools was ignored altogether.*

> *As the National Catholic Register's reporter Wayne Laugesenpoints out, the federal report said 422,000 California public-school students*

> would be victims before graduation — a number that dwarfs the state's entire Catholic-school enrollment of 143,000.

Protestants are worried as they know no institution is without its perpetrators. They feel lucky to an extent that they have not been called as has the Catholic Church and now of course Penn State University

I am not trying to create a controversy here between Catholics and protestants and K-12 public school teachers but the high-handed treatment of Penn State's innocent student body and athletes and State College as well as the defamation of Coach Paterno without a trial seems out of step with how the media and the pundits handle situations in other institutions.

> *There is an extensive report by Kathryn Joyce, from Prospect.org called "The Next Christian Sex Abuse Scandal." It is an eye opener to the extent of the sexual abuse epidemic in many Protestant Churches and schools. By this article, we do not want to undermine Catholic abuses by Catholic priests whom we feel should also be burned at the stake, but it is time to fess up, and before we pull the plank out of the eye in our Catholic brothers, Protestants should first see the plank in their eye."*

In other books, at this point, I offer several other concluding chapters in which I look at Joe Paterno as a human being and as a major asset to the Pennsylvania State University, and as a person who helped the University achieve its greatness. I suspect others may see it differently that's why there is very light treatment though the issues need to be mentioned because they happened right here at Linebacker U.

The damage to children in the Penn State sexual abuse situation cannot be minimized. That is not my issue, but a witch hunt intended to defame Penn State University and Joe Paterno and the football program by those in America who are frightened by success, is not an appropriate response to the problem.

Jerry Sandusky has been found guilty. Amen! The facts have apparently spoken and unless we plan to close down every public school and fire every principal whose charges went off on their own, then destroying the value of a Penn State experience and a Penn State education should be off the table.

Now, let's get off the subject of why Bill O'Brien became the coach and concentrate on his first season.

Games of the 2012 PSU Football Season

On September 1, at Beaver Stadium, the Nittany Lions unexpectedly lost to the Ohio University Bobcats L (14-24) as the Lions were trying to recover from a bad dream. The Bobcats obviously were not the same old pushover Bobcats.

They had changed under the guidance of Frank Solich. The whole Ohio football program enjoyed a return to national prominence in 2006, and in 2012 they beat Penn State and won their next six games. Tough to take the loss but a worthy opponent nonetheless.

Bill O'Brien recorded his first victory as Penn State's head coach when the Nittany Lions defeated Navy, 34-7, at Beaver Stadium on September 15, 2012.

2013 Penn State Football Season Coach Bill O'Brien

The 2013 Penn State Nittany Lions football team was coached by Bill O'Brien and the team was a member of the Big Ten Conference and its Leaders Division. Penn State was ineligible to play in a bowl game for the 2013 season, the second season of a four-year ban, due to NCAA sanctions imposed in the wake of the Jerry Sandusky sex abuse scandal. The NCAA should first investigate itself.

Before the season, Penn State needed to find a starting quarterback. They had an open competition between true freshman Christian Hackenberg won and started all 12 games for the Nittany Lions. Hackenberg had been ESPN's top-rated passer of the 2013 class. He beat out junior college quarterback Tyler Ferguson for the job

Despite sanctions, PSU still was able to recruit some stars though many chose to stake their fortunes elsewhere. Hackenberg headlined the 2013 recruiting class, which also featured tight end Adam Breneman. Breneman of course had a nice 2013 as a true freshman but injured himself as a sophomore, missed the 2014 season completely, and never really was able to play right again. After achieving his degree, he retired from football following the season due to a chronic knee injury.

John Butler was named Penn State's new defensive coordinator upon the departure of Ted Roof. Most predicted Penn State would have a similar season to that of the 2012 team, which won eight games and lost four, but there was uncertainty, as injuries were a big part of the season. PSU was thin in many positions because of the sanctions including offensive line and linebacker.

At the end of the season, Coach O'Brien, who did his best with two NCAA handicapped PSU teams accepted the head coaching position with the Houston Texans, leaving the Nittany Lions after two seasons. Early in 2014, the Nittany Lions hired James Franklin to replace O'Brien as head coach for the 2014 season.

Bill O'Brien was one of those special coaches that only are discovered every so often. Despite NCAA sanctions including limited scholarships and a bowl ban, He and his recruiting team retained their top recruit: quarterback Christian Hackenberg. Additional, PSU finished with the 24th ranked recruiting class according to ESPN, who cited retention of top prospects Hackenberg and tight end Adam Breneman, as well as adding depth in the secondary, overall giving them a "B" rating. Not bad for a team that many had completely minimized.

Coming off an 8–4 season during which attrition took its toll on overall prospects as nobody can win National Championships without well-gifted backup players, many college football pundits and analysts expected the Nittany Lions to perform similarly in 2013. There was the realization that since they were running thin on talent at the start, the season outlook could change quickly if the team was hampered by injuries. Then again, PSU could surprise everyone and win more games than they did in 2012. The results are in and it was more former than latter.

Allen Robinson (8) catches the ball at the one yard line to set up the game tying touchdown at the end of the fourth quarter of a game against Michigan at Beaver Stadium on Saturday, Oct. 12, 2013. Penn State beat Michigan in quadruple overtime, 43-40.

On October 12, at home, PSU beat a stubborn Michigan Team in 4 OT periods, W (43-40).

Chapter 20 James Franklin Era 2014 - 2018+

Coach # 16

2014	James Franklin 7-6	(2-6 Big Ten)
2015	James Franklin 7-6	(4-4 Big Ten)
2016	James Franklin 11-3	(8-2 Big Ten)
2017	James Franklin 7-6	(4-4 Big Ten)
2016	James Franklin 11-3	(8-2 Big Ten)
2019	James Franklin	

2014 Penn State Football Season Coach James Franklin

The 2014 Penn State Nittany Lions football team was led by first year head-coach James Franklin and played its home games in Beaver Stadium in University Park, Pennsylvania. It continued as a member of the Big Ten Conference and played in the newly organized East Division. As in 2011 through 2013, Penn State was ineligible to play in a bowl game due to NCAA sanctions. However, on September 8,

2014, the NCAA announced that Penn State would again be eligible for post-season games, effective immediately.

The Nittany Lions had a 7–6 overall record for the season with a 2–6 Big Ten mark, placing sixth in the Big Ten East Division. The Nittany Lions respectably concluded the season with a victory in the Pinstripe Bowl over Boston

Penn State qualified for one of the new Bowl games after Bowl Sanctions were lifted. On December 27 at 4:30 PM, Penn State played a feisty Boston College team in Yankee Stadium in the Bronx, NY and beat the Eagles in OT W (31-30). The game was also aired on ESPN. Overall, at 7-6, a recovering Penn State program had not yet gone negative without JoePa.

2015 Penn State Football Season Coach James Franklin

The 2015 Penn State Nittany Lions football team was led by second year head-coach James Franklin. The Nittany Lions finished the season 7–6; (4–4 in Big Ten) to finish in fourth place in the East Division of the Big Ten. They were invited to the TaxSlayer Bowl where the Lions lost to Georgia in a close battle L (17-24).

Penn State under James Franklin had two identical 7-6 seasons counting this bowl loss. There was a difference however, in that this year, PSU did 100% better when playing conference games (4-4).

With Joe Paterno having just one really dark period—even during his worst period, he would come back after rebuilding and pound the opposition. The fans were all looking for James Franklin to pull a JoePa in 2016.

2016 Penn State Football Season Coach James Franklin

The 2016 Penn State Nittany Lions football team was led by third year head-coach James Franklin. It played its home games in Beaver Stadium in University Park, Pennsylvania. The Penn State Nittany Lions are a member of the East Division of the Big Ten Conference.

The PSU 2016 schedule consisted of 7 home and 5 away games in the regular season. The Nittany Lions hosted Big Ten foes Iowa,

Maryland, Michigan State, Minnesota, and Ohio State, and traveled to Indiana, Michigan, Purdue, and Rutgers.

The team also hosted two of the three non–conference games which are against the Kent State Golden Flashes from the Mid-American Conference (MAC), Pittsburgh Panthers from the Atlantic Coast Conference (ACC), and the Temple Owls from the American Athletic Conference (AAC).

The Nittany Lions began the season slowly at 2–2. However, after losing to the Michigan Wolverines in game 4, they won nine straight conference games. This string of victories included defeating the Wisconsin Badgers in the Big Ten Championship Game. They represented the Big Ten in the 2017 Rose Bowl and were defeated by the Trojans of Southern California L (49-52) in a nail biter.

Penn State had its best season since Joe Paterno's 2009 season.

Date	Opponent	Site
September 3	Kent State*	Beaver Stadium • W(33-12)
September 10	at Pittsburgh	Heinz Field • L(39-42)
September 17	Temple	Beaver Stadium • W(34-27)
September 24	...at Michigan	Michigan Stadium • L(10-49)
October 1	Minnesota	Beaver Stadium • W(29-26)
October 8	Maryland	Beaver Stadium • W(38-14)
October 22	Ohio State	Beaver Stadium • W(24-21)
October 29	at Purdue	Ross–Ade Stadium • W(62-24)
November 5	Iowa	Beaver Stadium • W(41-14)
November 12	at Indiana	Memorial Stadium • W(45-31)
November 19	at Rutgers	High Point Solutions W(39-0)
November 26	Michigan State	Beaver Stadium • W(45-12)
December 3	Wisconsin	Lucas Oil Stadium W (38-31)
January 2	USC	Rose Bowl L (49-52)

2016 Season Highlights

Penn State had its best season since Joe Paterno's 2009 season brought the Nittany Lions 11 victories. It was quite a year for Penn State Fans and it was a long-time coming. How can anybody argue with the year--Big Ten Champions with 11 wins and a #5 ranking in the country. In fact, there was actually an outside shot that the Nittany Lions would be playing for a national title in 2016. For many, it was difficult to believe., Penn State is finally back! Go Lions!

* Below Photo by Rich Barnes

The last time the Lions had 11 wins was in 2009, which ended in a win over LSU in the Capital One Bowl... That team was loaded with NFL talent...but mostly on defense. Guys like Navorro Bowman, Sean Lee, Jared Odrick, Nate Stupar, and Jack Crawford all went on to have NFL careers.

Success for a team most often has to do with its coaching in combination with a fine quarterback. PSU had both in 2016 as Coach Franklin finally became comfortable with the team and the pressure. Trace McSorley was simply outstanding. It was a season that was fun to watch.

The Rose Bowl was very winnable and PSU had already showed its mettle when the Lions were down 28-7 and came back to beat Wisconsin in the B1G 10 Championship Game. PSU could have tucked away the Rose Bowl if the D could have come together a bit better.

The recent-old PSU looked like it was here again when the Nittany Lions played Michigan early in the season. It was as if the Lions were unprepared and Michigan was on key for the whole game. Big loss. Big number of points for Michigan and just 10 for PSU. It was demoralizing.

Barkley got just 59 yards on 15 carries. McSorley did not have it that day throwing for 121 yards, a TD, and a pick. Four different Michigan running backs had touchdown runs. It was tough to watch. Pitt created some jitters but did not ruin the season as the Lions came through in the end.

Nobody can say the Rose Bowl was not a great contest but the end of the Rose Bowl game was a big disappointment. The Nittany Lions were winning 49 to 45 and had the ball four times in the fourth quarter and did nothing.

Final scores matter and USC put it together to beat Penn State as the defense was not fully there for the last quarter. The pundits put the blame for the loss on coaches Franklin and Moorehead. There's nothing like great play calling at the end of a game. Didn't happen! Many are looking towards 2017 as a breakaway year but are concerned that there are a lot of great teams to get through. If the Defense can play a lot better, PSU has a chance to light up the scoreboard at will and that means a great season. We'll see!

Let's give PSU a big mental hug for a great 2016.

Let's hope for more in 2017.

Amen!

Who is Coach James Franklin?

A quick response would be that he is the guy who coached PSU to a Big Ten Championship in 2016 and who almost brought home a Rose Bowl Victory. Coach Franklin is our coach! There is more to it.

Just like the Penn State Community now knows, Coach Franklin's wife Fumi and their two daughters know that their husband and father is something special. Addy and Shola Franklin, however do not seem to understand how so many people happen to know their dad.

Head Coach James Franklin greets his daughters, Addy (left) and Shola (right), and his wife, Fumi, before the game against UMass on September 20, 2014.

When the Franklins are out walking the streets of State College, it's not uncommon for strangers to greet the coach with a wave and a "hello."

Most people see head football coach James Franklin as the man who leads the Nittany Lions out of the south tunnel at Beaver Stadium every Saturday in the fall.

But to his daughters, he's just dad.

I for one like that an awful lot!

On January 11, 2014 Penn State announced that it had selected James Franklin to lead its successful football program for the future.

The then new Nittany Lions' 17th head coach had previously led Vanderbilt to unprecedented success in his three years with the team

Franklin is one of the nation's most successful and dynamic coaches. Though he is the 16th season-long appointed permanent head football coach in its storied 130-year history, Tom Bradley actually has the title of 16th head coach as he served interim along with Joe Paterno in the 2011 season.

Franklin had won nine games in each of the past two years, and finished in the Top 25 in consecutive seasons with Vanderbilt. He knows how to coach. Both of these marked the first time in Vandy school history.

Franklin succeeds Bill O'Brien, who had a successful but short tenure at Penn State. He was named head coach of the National Football League's Houston Texans earlier in January 2014. Coach O'Brien is doing fine with Houston.

The new coach hails from Langhorne, Pa., a Philadelphia suburb. Coach Franklin's enthusiasm and tireless efforts resulted in taking Vanderbilt to new heights over the past three years, posting a 24-15 record, including marks of 9-4 during each of the past two seasons, capped by bowl victories. The Commodores finished the 2013 season with five consecutive victories, with wins over Florida, Georgia, Tennessee and Kentucky in Southeastern Conference play, along with a win over Houston in the BBVA Compass Bowl. Franklin's 2012 VU squad finished the season with seven consecutive victories and posted Vanderbilt's first nine-win season since 1915.

"Coach Franklin's record of success is extraordinary, but even more impressive is his passion for not only the game of football, but also creating an atmosphere in which student-athletes can succeed. His character, work ethic, values and knowledge of the game make him an outstanding fit for our program and to lead our student-athletes."

Penn State and Vanderbilt annually rank among the nation's top institutions in the graduation of its football student-athletes. In the NCAA Graduation Success Rate data from October 2013, the Nittany Lions and Commodores both ranked among the leaders in the Football Bowl Subdivision.

Penn State's 85 percent Graduation Success Rate was tied for 12th among the nation's 124 FBS programs and Vanderbilt's 82 percent GSR was tied for the best in the Southeastern Conference. Both programs were well above the 70 percent FBS graduation rate average.

A two-time All-Pennsylvania State Athletic Conference (PSAC) quarterback at East Stroudsburg University, prior to Penn State, Franklin had already demonstrated the ability to recruit, teach and motivate talented student-athletes throughout his coaching tenure.

He was named Vanderbilt's head coach on Dec. 17, 2010, after three years as the assistant head coach/offensive coordinator/quarterbacks' coach at Maryland, his second stint with the Terps.

Franklin also served as the offensive coordinator and quarterbacks' coach at Kansas State in 2006-07 and the wide receivers coach of the NFL's Green Bay Packers (2005) prior to arriving in Nashville.

"I can't tell you how excited I am to come home," Franklin said. "I grew up watching Penn State football and now to be at the helm of such a storied program is a tremendous honor. It's important to me to be a part of a University that strives for excellence in everything they do. When football student-athletes come to Penn State, they have a unique opportunity to receive a premium education while playing at the highest level of competition.

"I'm incredibly excited to get to know the students, alumni, and fans who have demonstrated such loyalty to the University as a whole and to the football program in particular," Franklin added. "I've worked my way through every division of football and no other school boasts a fan base like we do.

2017 Penn State Football Season Coach James Franklin   Fiesta Bowl Win

The 2017 Penn State Nittany Lions football team was led by fourth year head-coach James Franklin. Pennsylvania State University played in the 2017 NCAA Division I FBS. It played its home games in Beaver Stadium in University Park, Pennsylvania. The Penn State Nittany Lions are a member of the East Division of the Big Ten Conference.

The Nittany Lions entered the season as defending Big Ten champions, and were ranked sixth in the preseason AP Poll. The team won its first seven games by an average margin of victory of 30 points. One of the highlights was a 42–13 pounding of #19 Michigan, and a rise to second in the AP Poll. Penn State had a close match against #6 Ohio State in a highly anticipated road match-losing by a score of 38–39. Then they fell gain the next week on the road to Michigan State. That was their last loss of the season.

They finished the regular season tied for second in the East Division with a conference record of 7–2. They were invited to the 2017 Fiesta Bowl, where they defeated Washington, and finished the season at 11–2 and ranked eighth in the final polls.

The team was at the top of its game throughout the season much like the Paterno years. The offense was led by running back Saquon

Barkley and quarterback Trace McSorley. Barkley topped the conference with 18 rushing touchdowns along with 1,271 rushing yards. He was named a consensus first-team All-American as an all-purpose back. McSorely's 3,571 passing yards and 284 pass completions also led the conference. On defense, safety Marcus Allen was named first-team all-conference by the coaches. It was no championship but it was a great year.

2017 Fiesta Bowl

PSU beat Washington in the Fiesta Bowl off the great plays of Trace McSorley who was an amazing 12-of-12 with a 290 QB rating on 3rd downs. Amazing.
Penn State grabbed its second 11-win season in a row by beating Washington at the Fiesta Bowl, 35-28. This may have looked like a close game but the Nittany Lions literally pounded the Huskies 545-331 in total yardage. Penn State was simply great thanks to quarterback Trace McSorley and his cast of receivers.

Some figures to put his game into context include 13-of-17 (76 percent) as Penn State's total conversion rate on third downs FYI, the national average is 40 percent. Penn State's season conversion rate entering the day was 44 percent, while Washington's defense had given up 34 percent.

Penn State had a strong 6.1 average yards to gain on third downs. Third-and-mediums are supposed to be difficult, but the Nittany Lions made them look like nothing. In the game, McSorley had two third-down TD passes to receiver DaeSean Hamilton, including this 48-yarder (picture on next page) that opened the game's scoring in the first quarter. Bravo Penn State.:

2018 Penn State Football Season Coach James Franklin   Citrus Bowl Loss

The 2018 Penn State Nittany Lions football team was led by fifth-year head-coach James Franklin. Pennsylvania State University played in the 2018 NCAA Division I FBS. It played its home games in Beaver Stadium in University Park, Pennsylvania. The Penn State Nittany Lions are a member of the East Division of the Big Ten Conference. They were a member of the East Division of the Big Ten Conference.

Penn State was coming off an 11–2, Fiesta Bowl-winning season in 2017. They began the year at 10th in the preseason AP Poll. They narrowly escaped an upset in their first game of the year by defeating Appalachian State in overtime. These smaller schools often are so excited to play powerhouses that they pull off victories. Not this time but close.

The Nittany Lions won their first four games and entered an anticipated home game against No. 4 Ohio State at No. 9, but lost to the Buckeyes by a score of 26–27. The following week the team was upset by Michigan State on homecoming. The Lions rebounded with a home win against then-No. 18 Iowa, but they were blown out the following week by Michigan 42–7. The Nittany Lions finished the regular season in third in the Big Ten East with a conference record of 6–3. They were invited to the Citrus Bowl, where they lost to Kentucky to finish the year at 9–4.

Senior quarterback Trace McSorley led the team in passing, finishing with 2,530 passing yards and 18 passing touchdowns to go along with 12 rushing touchdowns. He was named second team All-Big Ten by both the media and coaches. McSorely became the all-time school record holder in several categories, including career passing yards, completions, passing touchdowns, and total touchdowns responsible for (however best that is said).

Junior running back Miles Sanders helped the team by finishing in second in the conference in rushing with 1,274 yards. On defense, cornerback Amani Oruwariye and lineman Yetur Gross-Matos were named first-team all-conference by the media. Penn State performed well but this was a long way from undefeated and untied and a long way from a championship But, with Franklin at the helm, there is more to com.

We Are...Penn State!!"

Bravo Coach Franklin. Please keep up the good work!

God bless you Coach Franklin.

We all mean it!

That's All Folks!
This book focuses on PSU Football. The author has not included stories about the scandal. PSU is much more than that. Thank you for choosing this book among the many that are in your option list. I sincerely appreciate it Five new PSU titles have been released since the original version of this book. See list on inside back cover—next page: amazon.com/author/brianwkelly

Other Books by Brian W. Kelly: (amazon.com, and Kindle)

Hope for Wilkes-Barre-John Q. Doe Next Mayor Wilkes-Barre PA: John Doe Plan, help create better city!
Democrat Secret for Power & Winning Elections: Open borders & amnesty & millions of new Dem Voters
The Cowardly Congress Whatever happened to Congress doing the work of the people?
Help for Mayor George and Next Mayor of Wilkes-Barre How to vote for the next Mayor &Council
Ghost of Wilkes-Barre Future: Spirit's advice for residents about how to pick the next Mayor and Council
Great Players in Air Force Football: Air Force's best players of all time
Great Coaches in Air Force Football: From Coach 1 to Coach Troy Calhoun
Great Moments in Air Force Football: From day 1 to today
Great Players in Navy Football: Navy's best including Bellino & Staubach
Great Coaches in Navy Football: From Coach 1 to Coach #39 Ken Niumatalolo
Great Moments in Navy Football: From day 1 to coach Ken Niumatalolo l
No Tree! No Toys! No Toot Toot! Heartwarming story. Christmas gone while 19 month old napped
How to End DACA, Sanctuary Cities, & Resident Illegal Aliens . best solution to wipe shadows in America.
Government Must Stop Ripping Off Seniors' Social Security!: Hey buddy, seniors can no longer spare a dime?
Special Report: Solving America's Student Debt Crisis!: The only real solution to the $1.52 Trillion debt
How to End DACA, Sanctuary Cities, & Resident Illegal Aliens . best solution to wipe shadows in America.
The Winning Political Platform for America Unique winning approach to solve big problems in America.
Lou Barletta v Bob Casey for US Senate Barletta's unique approach to solving big problems in America.
John Chrin v Matt Cartwright for Congress Chrin has a unique approach to solve big problems in America.
The Cure for Hate !!! Can the cure be any worse than this disease that is crippling America?
Andrew Cuomo's Time to Go? "He Was Never that Great!": Cuomo says America never that great
White People Are Bad! Bad! Bad! Whoever thought a popular slogan in 2018 would be *It's OK to be White!*
The Fake News Media Is Also Corrupt !!!: Fake press / media today is not worthy to be 4th Estate.
God Gave US Donald Trump? Trump was sent from God as the people's answer
Millennials Say America Was "Never That Great": Too many pleased days of political chumps not over!
White People Are Bad! Bad! Bad! In 2018, too many people find race as a non-equalizer.
It's Time for The John Doe Party… Don't you think? By By Elephants.
Great Players in Florida Gators Football… Tim Tebow and a ton of other great players
Great Coaches in Florida Gators Football… The best coaches in Gator history.
The Constitution by Hamilton, Jefferson, Madison, et al. The Real Constitution
The Constitution Companion. Will help you learn and understand the Constitution
Great Coaches in Clemson Football The best Clemson Coaches right to Dabo Swinney
Great Players in Clemson Football The best Clemson players in history
Winning Back America. America's been stolen and can be won back completely
The Founding of America… Great book to pick up a lot of great facts
Defeating America's Career Politicians. The scoundrels need to go.
Midnight Mass by Jack Lammers… You remember what it was like Great story
The Bike by Jack Lammers… Great heartwarming Story by Jack
Wipe Out All Student Loan Debt--Now! Watch the economy go boom!
No Free Lunch Pay Back Welfare! Why not pay it back?
Deport All Millennials Now!!! Why they deserve to be deported and/or saved
DELETE the EPA, Please! The worst decisions to hurt America
Taxation Without Representation 4th Edition Should we throw the TEA overboard again?
Four Great Political Essays by Thomas Dawson
Top Ten Political Books for 2018… Cliffnotes Version of 10 Political Books
Top Six Patriotic Books for 2018… Cliffnotes version of 6 Patriotic Boosk
Why Trump Got Elected!.. It's great to hear about a great milestone in America!
The Day the Free Press Died. Corrupt Press Lives on!
Solved (Immigration) The best solutions for 2018
Solved II (Obamacare, Social Security, Student Debt) Check it out; They're solved.
Great Moments in Pittsburgh Steelers Football… Six Super Bowls and more.
Great Players in Pittsburgh Steelers Football ,,,Chuck Noll, Bill Cowher, Mike Tomin, etc.
Great Coaches in New England Patriots Football,,, Bill Belichick the one and only plus others
Great Players in New England Patriots Football… Tom Brady, Drew Bledsoe et al.
Great Coaches in Philadelphia Eagles Football..Andy Reid, Doug Pederson & Lots more
Great Players in Philadelphia Eagles Football Great players such as Sonny Jurgensen
Great Coaches in Syracuse Football All the greats including Ben Schwartzwalder
Great Players in Syracuse Football. Highlights best players such as Jim Brown & Donovan McNabb
Millennials are People Too !!! Give US millennials help to live American Dream
Brian Kelly for the United States Senate from PA: Fresh Face for US Senate
The Candidate's Bible. Don't pray for your campaign without this bible
Rush Limbaugh's Platform for Americans… Rush will love it
Sean Hannity's Platform for Americans… Sean will love it
Donald Trump's New Platform for Americans. Make Trump unbeatable in 2020

Tariffs Are Good for America! One of the best tools a president can have
Great Coaches in Pittsburgh Steelers Football Sixteen of the best coaches ever to coach in pro football.
Great Moments in New England Patriots Football Great football moments from Boston to New England
Great Moments in Philadelphia Eagles Football. The best from the Eagles from the beginning of football.
Great Moments in Syracuse Football The great moments, coaches & players in Syracuse Football
Boost Social Security Now! Hey Buddy Can You Spare a Dime?
The Birth of American Football. From the first college game in 1869 to the last Super Bowl
Obamacare: A One-Line Repeal Congress must get this done.
A Wilkes-Barre Christmas Story A wonderful town makes Christmas all the better
A Boy, A Bike, A Train, and a Christmas Miracle A Christmas story that will melt your heart
Pay-to-Go America-First Immigration Fix
Legalizing Illegal Aliens Via Resident Visas Americans-first plan saves $Trillions. Learn how!
60 Million Illegal Aliens in America!!! A simple, America-first solution.
The Bill of Rights By Founder James Madison Refresh *your knowledge of the specific rights for all*
Great Players in Army Football Great Army Football played by great players..
Great Coaches in Army Football Army's coaches are all great.
Great Moments in Army Football Army Football at its best.
Great Moments in Florida Gators Football Gators Football from the start. This is the book.
Great Moments in Clemson Football CU Football at its best. This is the book.
Great Moments in Florida Gators Football Gators Football from the start. This is the book.
The Constitution Companion. A Guide to Reading and Comprehending the Constitution
The Constitution by Hamilton, Jefferson, & Madison – Big type and in English
PATERNO: The Dark Days After Win # 409. Sky began to fall within days of win # 409.
JoePa 409 Victories: Say No More! Winningest Division I-A football coach ever
American College Football: The Beginning From before day one football was played.
Great Coaches in Alabama Football Challenging the coaches of every other program!
Great Coaches in Penn State Football the Best Coaches in PSU's football program
Great Players in Penn State Football The best players in PSU's football program
Great Players in Notre Dame Football The best players in ND's football program
Great Coaches in Notre Dame Football The best coaches in any football program
Great Players in Alabama Football from Quarterbacks to offensive Linemen Greats!
Great Moments in Alabama Football AU Football from the start. This is the book.
Great Moments in Penn State Football PSU Football, start--games, coaches, players,
Great Moments in Notre Dame Football ND Football, start, games, coaches, players
Cross Country with the Parents A great trip from East Coast to West with the kids
Seniors, Social Security & the Minimum Wage. Things seniors need to know.
How to Write Your First Book and Publish It with CreateSpace. You too can be an author.
The US Immigration Fix--It's all in here. Finally, an answer.
I had a Dream IBM Could be #1 Again The title is self-explanatory
WineDiets.Com Presents The Wine Diet Learn how to lose weight while having fun.
Wilkes-Barre, PA; Return to Glory Wilkes-Barre City's return to glory
Geoffrey Parsons' Epoch... The Land of Fair Play Better than the original.
The Bill of Rights 4 Dummmies! This is the best book to learn about your rights.
Sol Bloom's Epoch ...Story of the Constitution The best book to learn the Constitution
America 4 Dummmies! All Americans should read to learn about this great country.
The Electoral College 4 Dummmies! How does it really work?
The All-Everything Machine Story about IBM's finest computer server.
ThankYou IBM! This book explains how IBM was beaten in the computer marketplace by neophytes

Amazon.com/author/brianwkelly
Brian W. Kelly has written 207 books. Thank you for buying this one.
Other Kelly books can be found at amazon.com/author/brianwkelly

www.ingramcontent.com/pod-product-compliance
Lightning Source LLC
Chambersburg PA
CBHW071658090426
42738CB00009B/1572